BY MICOL NEGRIN

The Best Pasta Sauces: Favorite Regional Italian Recipes

Rustico: Regional Italian Country Cooking

The Italian Grill: Fresh Ideas to Fire Up Your Outdoor Cooking

The Best Pasta Sauces

THE BEST
PASTA SAUCES

Favorite Regional Italian Recipes

MICOL NEGRIN

BALLANTINE BOOKS · NEW YORK

Published in the United States by Ballantine Books, an imprint of Random House, a division of Random House LLC, a Penguin Random House Company, New York.

BALLANTINE and the HOUSE colophon are registered trademarks of Random House LLC.

Photography by Dino De Angelis

Wine pairings by Costas Mouzouras

Negrin, Micol.
  The best pasta sauces : favorite regional Italian recipes / Micol Negrin.—First edition.
    pages cm
  Includes index.
  ISBN 978-0-345-54714-9 (hardback)—ISBN 978-0-345-54715-6 (ebook)
  1. Sauces. 2. Cooking, Italian. I. Title.
  TX819.A1N44 2014
  641.81'4—dc23   2014017531

Printed in Hong Kong on acid-free paper

www.ballantinebooks.com

9 8 7 6 5 4 3 2 1

First Edition

Book design by Liz Cosgrove

Contents

INTRODUCTION viii

THE TEN RULES OF COOKING PASTA x

SERVING PASTA ITALIAN-STYLE xii

PASTA SAUCES IN THE ITALIAN KITCHEN xv

NORTHERN ITALY

Val d'Aosta, Piedmont, Liguria, Lombardy, Trentino–Alto Adige, Friuli–Venezia Giulia, the Veneto, Emilia-Romagna   1

CENTRAL ITALY

The Marches, Tuscany, Umbria, Latium   89

SOUTHERN ITALY

Abruzzo, Molise, Apulia, Campania, Basilicata, Calabria   130

THE ISLANDS

Sicily, Sardinia   197

BASIC RECIPES   220

MAIL-ORDER SOURCES 229

ACKNOWLEDGMENTS 231

INDEX 233

Introduction

A BRIEF HISTORY OF PASTA

Legend has it that Marco Polo discovered noodles on his voyage to China—but nothing could be further from the truth. Pasta had already been a staple in the Mediterranean since the Neolithic era, about eight thousand years ago. The Etruscans (who lived in the tenth century BCE in what is now Tuscany, Umbria, and Latium), as well as the ancient Romans, Greeks, and Arabs, were preparing wheat-based noodles some three thousand years ago. At the necropolis of Cerveteri, an ancient Etruscan city, there are carvings of the tools needed for pasta making (rolling pins, cutters, and boards for rolling the dough) dating to the fourth century BCE. The Roman epicure Apicius described the making of *lagane* (similar to lasagna, either boiled or baked) and many pasta sauces in his fourth-century book, *De Re Coquinaria*, and in the twelfth century, the Arab geographer Al-Idrisi wrote about the mills of the town of Trabia, just twenty miles from Palermo in Sicily, where a long, thin pasta known as *itryah* was made using flour and water for dispatch across the Mediterranean.

Most of the pasta eaten in Italy in ancient times was placed raw in sauce and baked in the oven, without being boiled first. In the Middle Ages, this changed, and new pasta shapes were introduced: some were short, some were filled, and, most important, the art of drying pasta was developed, likely introduced on behest of the Arabs who had settled in Sicily and required staple foods for their long journeys in the desert.

Small shops specializing in pasta opened in Naples and Genoa, as well as in Sicily, and eventually spread across Italy. By the 1300s, Italian pasta-makers had formed guilds. Most significantly, by the 1700s industrial production of pasta began in earnest, making dried pasta available and affordable for more Italians than ever before.

Tomatoes, a New World food, were initially planted as ornamentals rather than as food in Italy. Many botanists thought them poisonous, as they belong to the Solanaceae (or nightshade) family, which includes several toxic plants. It took nearly two centuries before tomatoes became a common ingredient on Italian tables. In the 1700s, tomatoes and pasta became a common pairing, as techniques for growing, processing, and preserving tomatoes progressed alongside the industrial production of pasta. The first tomatoes brought to Italy were likely a yellow variety (hence their name, *pomodoro*, which translates as "golden apple"). But before the 1700s, those who could afford to eat pasta often sauced it in ways we would not recognize (or perhaps approve of) today: in ancient Rome, intensely savory ingredients like fermented fish sauce (known as *garum* or *liquamen*) formed the basis of the sauce for fried, boiled, or baked noodles; in the Middle Ages and Renaissance, sweet and salty essences intermingled (honey and black pepper, for instance, or reduced wine and fragrant spices like cumin or rue).

With the advent of industrial pasta production and the spread of pasta to peasant homes, sauces for pasta began to take on many guises. Olive oil or butter, perhaps with grated cheese or toasted bread crumbs, became a common preparation. Boiled vegetables or bits of salted or dried meat and fish were welcome additions. Feast days and banquets called for extravagant pastas featuring slowly simmered meat sauces or rich ragùs.

Today, if you travel across Italy, you can still find echoes of the medieval and Renaissance sweet sauces, especially at Christmas, when nuts, sugar, and cinnamon frequently lend festive flavor to pastas. You'll also find echoes of the spice trade that fueled much of the Italian economy in centuries past in pasta sauces that call for nutmeg, cinnamon, poppy seeds, caraway seeds, and other spices. But what you'll find most of all is a tremendous variety of sauces that draw on the bounty of land and sea, on the ingenuity of the home cook, and on the imperative of letting the pasta itself be the star of the plate. No sauce is so intense as to mask the pasta it is served with. No sauce is so plentiful as to drown the pasta it is tossed with. The sauce is merely a vehicle for enjoying the pasta, and it is a vehicle that changes marvelously from region to region, depending on what local cooks can find in their gardens and on what has informed their cooking over the centuries.

I invite you to join me as we travel across Italy's twenty regions for a taste of the country's most glorious pasta sauces. It is a journey that might surprise you, just as it did me, as you discover unexpected flavor combinations. And it is a journey that will hopefully inspire you, as you experience the seemingly never-ending, always fascinating, and relentlessly delicious world of Italian pasta and sauces.

The Ten Rules of Cooking Pasta

1. First of all, start with a deep, tall pot. Don't use a saucepan for cooking your pasta, and there is no need for nonstick cookware unless you happen to only have a nonstick stockpot. I suggest a deep stockpot with a colander insert; this will make draining the pasta and reserving some of the pasta cooking water much easier later (no more running to the sink with a boiling pot of water to find a colander; plus, this sort of pot comes in handy when making pasta that is cooked along with vegetables).

2. Bring 4 cups of water to a boil for every 4 ounces of pasta you intend to cook. The water should be at a rolling boil when you add the pasta, or the pasta won't cook through evenly.

3. Add at least 1 teaspoon of salt per quart of water after the water comes to a boil (if you add it earlier, it will raise the boiling temperature of the water and make the water come to a boil more slowly). The water should be very salty; not all of the salt will penetrate the pasta, but rather it will flavor the water, so the pasta will not be too salty once drained.

4. Never add oil to the cooking water! The pasta won't stick together unless you forget to stir it often as it cooks. (Adding oil to the water will create a slippery surface on the pasta; the sauce will adhere poorly to the pasta when it's time to combine the two.)

5. Add the pasta to the boiling water all at once, and stir with a long-handled spoon that will allow you to reach all the way to the bottom of the pot. If you are making long pasta, keep stirring until it becomes supple, loses rigidity, and is entirely submerged in the water. If you aren't careful when cooking long pasta, you may end up leaving parts of it hanging out of the water for minutes, resulting in unevenly cooked pasta; take the time to push all of the pasta strands into the boiling water, and do it as quickly as possible so the pasta cooks evenly.

6. Keep the water boiling the whole time as the pasta cooks: if the water does not return to a rolling boil quickly, cover the pot with a lid after adding the pasta to the boiling water. If the pasta water is not boiling, the outside of the pasta will be overcooked by the time the inside is al dente. The only case where you don't want water at a rolling boil is when cooking filled pastas such as ravioli or tortellini, as the filling may leak out; in this case, keep the water at a low boil.

7. Stir the pasta every 30 seconds or so. This is crucial to prevent sticking and to ensure even cooking. And don't forget to reach all the way to the bottom of the pot when stirring.

8. Taste often to see if the pasta is almost fully cooked, and drain it when it's al dente (meaning "to the tooth," because it should offer a little bite when it's drained): there should still be a tiny white dot at the center. Fresh pasta may cook very quickly (in as little as 1 minute for delicate, thin pasta), so never walk out of the kitchen when cooking pasta. Dried pasta takes anywhere from 8 to 14 minutes, depending on the thickness and shape (except angel hair pasta, which cooks in a minute or two); start tasting the pasta about 2 minutes prior to the suggested cooking time on the box. You can always cook pasta longer, but you can't "uncook" pasta that is overcooked. When cooking angel hair pasta, taste for doneness 30 seconds after it has been added to the boiling water.

9. Reserve about 2 cups of the pasta cooking water before you drain the pasta. Use as much of this reserved pasta cooking water as needed to thin out your sauce (this allows you to cut down on olive oil or butter). Also, because the pasta cooking water is so rich in starch, it helps the sauce bind to the pasta, making for a lovely, velvety quality. And the residual heat in the reserved pasta cooking water will help your pasta stay hot longer.

10. *Never* rinse pasta after you drain it, even if you plan to serve the pasta cold: rinsing pasta will wash out the starch and much of the flavor. (To cool drained pasta for use in cold dishes, toss it with a touch of olive oil and spread it out on a large tray until it reaches room temperature, about 15 minutes.)

Serving Pasta Italian-Style

In Italy, pasta is either a meal in itself or a first course. It is never a side dish to be served alongside protein or vegetables: it is the star of its own plate. There are many reasons for this. First and foremost, pasta has historically been the main source of nourishment, eaten once or twice a day since the late 1700s in most central and southern Italian regions, as well as in Sicily, to fill the belly and nourish the soul. (Many northern Italian regions often relied on bread, polenta, potatoes, or rice to fill that same void.) If the family was lucky, there would be a bit of animal protein on the table as well, but most Italians until the 1950s were perfectly content eating a large plate of pasta with some vegetables, olive oil, or even just toasted bread crumbs for flavor; dessert was reserved for feast days, as were significant portions of meat or fish. So pasta took a central role on the Italian table and was served as the main (if not the only) course more often than not.

Today, Italy is a rich country and Italians have many food choices available. Pasta may not always be the focal point and anchor of every meal, but when it is served, it is served on its own: the care and thought that go into making sauce for pasta dictate that the pasta be enjoyed without anything next to it to muddy or confuse the flavors.

A lot of students in my cooking classes ask me if they can just grill a piece of fish or meat and toss it with the pasta, or serve it on top of the pasta, to round out the meal and make it an all-in-one dish. Needless to say, this won't yield an authentically Italian eating experience: Italians never grill a piece of fish or chicken and serve it atop pasta. The flavors of any topping or sauce need to integrate into the pasta itself, in order to create a perfectly balanced and harmonious dish. So, for the sake of authenticity, I urge you not to add chicken or shrimp or another protein to the vegetarian sauce recipes in this book to "round out the meal" with some additional protein; that would alter the nature of the sauces. Instead, serve the protein of your choice as a second course, or skip the meat or fish altogether, especially if the sauce for the pasta contains protein from legumes, dairy, or even meat or fish.

So here is how to think of pasta as Italians do: you can either serve it as a main course, following it with a medley of vegetables or salad; or you can serve it as a first course prior to serving the protein main course and vegetable side dishes of your choosing. If you are serving pasta as a main course, you will want to serve four people (or six people with more moderate appetites) per pound of uncooked pasta; if you are serving it as a first course before a protein main course, you can plan on serving six people (or eight people with more moderate appetites) per pound of uncooked pasta. Nevertheless, all of the recipes in this book assume that you are serving pasta as a main course, so they are written to serve four people (or six people with more moderate appetites) per pound of uncooked pasta.

But how do you balance a menu that features pasta? Think of a balanced meal as one that contains both protein and vegetables. Protein need not come in the form of fish or meat—it can come from dairy or legumes—so even a vegetarian pasta that contains chickpeas, lentils, beans, cream, or cheese contains a good amount of protein. If you are serving pasta with a meat-based or fish-based sauce, you may want to follow it with a few cooked or raw vegetables; if you are serving a pasta with a vegetable sauce (such as Crushed Asparagus Sauce, page 151), you can serve a meat, fish, or legume-based protein to follow, along with some vegetables both raw and cooked. I do advocate eating vegetables in both their raw and cooked state at every meal, as this balances the richness of other more complicated dishes and provides necessary nutrients and vitamins. You are welcome to e-mail me for recipes for suggested main courses and side dishes if you wish through my website, www.rusticocooking.com.

Saucing Pasta the Italian Way

Remember that the way pasta combines with its sauce determines how good the final dish will be. First off, you need to cook the pasta properly (see page x); but once you've drained your perfectly al dente pasta, you need to sauce it, and that is an art in itself.

After draining the pasta, reserve about 2 cups of pasta cooking water to thin out the sauce as needed. You may not need all of it, but once you've thrown the pasta cooking water down the drain, you won't be able to get it back; water from the tap simply doesn't have the same starchy lusciousness to coat the pasta properly. Don't rinse the pasta after draining (you don't want to rob it of its starchy coating). For hot sauces, immediately add the drained pasta to a pan of simmering sauce. Ideally, all hot sauces should be in the pan, waiting for the drained pasta; the two will then be sautéed together for a minute or longer to mingle to perfection and create a perfectly sauced plate of pasta. Don't skip this sautéing step: it makes all the difference, and you'll want to add some of that reserved pasta cooking water to thin out the sauce as needed. The sauce should coat the pasta well, but the pasta should not be floating in sauce. The only pasta shape served hot that really should not be sautéed is gnocchi; these are often too delicate to hit a hot pan, so I prefer to sauce them in a wide bowl with the sauce, using a rubber spatula to gently combine. In the case of room-temperature, no-cook sauces such as pesto, add the drained pasta immediately to a deep bowl where the sauce awaits. Toss the pasta and sauce together, and add some of the reserved pasta cooking water as needed to get the sauce to coat the pasta properly.

Pasta is best enjoyed hot, with the exception of bean- or legume-based dishes: these are often even better when they sit a bit, as the flavors marry better.

Pairing Pasta Shapes with Their Ideal Sauce

And now, for the question everyone asks in my cooking classes: How do you know which pasta shape to pair with which sauce? Easy. Generally, long or flat noodles are better suited to creamy or smooth sauces; short or tubular shapes with ridges, nooks, and crannies work best with chunky sauces, because they catch the bits and pieces in their hollows. Heavy, robust sauces such as long-simmered ragùs tend to do better with thick-walled pastas such as cavatelli, rigatoni, or even gnocchi; delicate preparations, such as subtle fish-based sauces or pestos, marry better with thin, long, flat pastas such as linguine or tagliatelle. Regional Italian traditions too dictate certain pairings, but you are welcome to disagree with them: after all, you are cooking to please yourself and your dining companions. For example, in Rome, Spicy Tomato, Onion, and Guanciale Sauce (page 125) is usually served with bucatini, a hollow spaghetti, but I much prefer it with tagliatelle or even penne rigate or mezzi rigatoni, which seem to pick up the sauce better to my taste. What's really interesting is to see how a sauce tastes completely different on two different pasta shapes; so for each pasta sauce, I have suggested a few ideal pasta shapes to try.

Pasta Sauces in the Italian Kitchen

While many Americans tend to reach for tomato or cream when saucing pasta, the reality is that a great number of Italian pasta sauces do not rely on either of these ingredients. There are sauces based on vegetables; seafood; meat; cheese; nuts; and dried legumes and beans. There are even sauces without any liquid ingredients (except pasta cooking water and perhaps a little olive oil): for example, "Poor Man's" Garlic Bread Crumb Sauce (page 175), or sauces made from long-cooked vegetables (such as Silky Broccoli Raab, Garlic, and Crushed Red Pepper Sauce on page 179, or Crushed Asparagus Sauce on page 151). The latter family of sauces is especially interesting for busy cooks, because they often require remarkably few ingredients, need even fewer pots and pans, and are very healthful and quick to make.

So what exactly qualifies a sauce as a *pasta* sauce? Usually, pasta sauces aim to elevate the flavor of the pasta, never to mask it. Pasta sauces are never so intensely flavored or abundant as to overwhelm the pasta. Pasta sauces are usually fairly liquid, so as to better coat the pasta; they are rarely reduced to a glazing consistency, and seldom thickened with flour, unlike sauces for meat. Even when there are no liquid ingredients used per se (for example, Prosciutto di Parma and Parmigiano Sauce on page 84), pasta cooking water is added to ensure that each strand or piece of pasta is thoroughly coated with flavorful liquid and that the pasta will not stick together.

One of my favorite ways to sauce pasta is to boil vegetables directly with the pasta until they fall deliciously apart and create an unctuous coating that sauces the drained pasta (such as in Smashed Potato Sauce with Cracked Black Pepper and Olive Oil on page 98). This may not sound like a sauce, but as the vegetable breaks down into a purée, a natural sauce forms that coats the pasta beautifully once drained. Broccoli, broccoli raab, potatoes, asparagus, fava beans, and even peas can be transformed into a luscious purée after lengthy cooking.

A few pointers about preparing *battuto* (aromatic ingredients) in pasta sauces: mincing (rather than finely dicing or chopping) is very important in any sauce where you want to not be able to discern any pieces of carrot, onion, celery, sun-dried tomato—whatever you're using to lend flavor. These ingredients need to break down completely and meld into the sauce, where they essentially disappear from a textural standpoint. Mincing is more laborious but more traditional and much tastier. I always place aromatic ingredients and oil in a cold pan and then turn on the heat. I find that it extracts better flavor more gently, and with less risk of burning, than if one heats the pan, then heats the oil, then adds the aromatics (especially if one is using a thin-bottomed pan). Also, when using extra-virgin olive oil, which has a low smoke point, this is by the far the safer way to go. It is the traditional method for starting sauces in Italy.

One thing I've noticed when teaching students at our cooking school is that people underestimate the importance the pasta cooking water makes to the final texture and slipperiness of the sauce. Most students are surprised at how much of the pasta cooking water is stirred into the sauce. They tell me that at home, their pasta looks much drier than when we serve it; even their simmering sauces at home are more reduced than ours.

Think like an Italian when saucing your pasta: keep the sauce moist as it bubbles on the stove (you may need to add pasta cooking water repeatedly as it cooks), and add enough of the pasta cooking water to render the sauce slippery when serving. Remember that as pasta sits, it absorbs liquid, so the sauce will dry out further as it coats the pasta.

And one word of advice about cheese: not every pasta needs it, and some pasta dishes are better without it. As much as I love cheese, I don't add it to most legume and bean sauces, I avoid it on seafood and fish sauces, and I often skip it on vegetable-based sauces. Always try the pasta the way the recipe suggests; if cheese is not called for, this was a conscious decision on my part, and you shouldn't automatically sprinkle with cheese before tasting.

Northern Italy, Italy's largest and most prosperous area, is made up of Val d'Aosta, Piedmont, Liguria, Lombardy, Trentino–Alto Adige, Friuli–Venezia Giulia, the Veneto, and Emilia-Romagna. These regions border Switzerland and France to the northwest, Austria to the northeast, and Slovenia to the east, and their cuisine is marked to a certain extent by these countries' culinary influences. Cheeses in northern Italy are prevalently made from cow's milk, and it is here that Grana Padano and Parmigiano-Reggiano, Italy's most famous grating cheeses, are produced; as a result, most pasta sauces in the area rely heavily on these products, as well as on butter and fresh cream, for a rich mouthfeel and flavor.

NORTHERN ITALY

Val d'Aosta

Val d'Aosta, Italy's smallest region, shares a border with France and Switzerland. Not surprisingly, the region's cuisine is historically anchored in its mountainous terrain. Butter and cow's milk cheese are staples here, used in most preparations with abandon. Fontina is the most prized of all local cheeses; made from the milk of Alpine cows since the Middle Ages, it has a rich, buttery texture and an incredible ability to melt. In nearby Piedmont, pastas both dried and fresh constitute an important first course; but in Val d'Aosta, it is polenta and soup that appear most often on the family table. Pasta became part of the local cooking tradition only a few decades ago, introduced by Piedmontese merchants who settled in the valley after the Aosta-Turin railway was built. Pasta sauces tend to be simple affairs that make the most of a few key ingredients, and a handful of feast-day sauces call for marinating game from the mountains with red wine and aromatic vegetables, then slow-cooking to melt-in-the-mouth tenderness.

Creamy Fontina Sauce with Crushed Walnuts and White Truffle Oil

Fonduta con Noci al Tartufo This sauce is usually served over polenta or with bread in Val d'Aosta. A sumptuous take on fondue, it features milk, cream, Fontina, and butter and is finished with egg yolks and truffle oil; shaved white truffles over the top would be a lovely indulgence. SERVES 4

Ingredient notes: Walnuts (like all nuts and whole grains) are susceptible to rancidity due to their high fat content. Store them in the freezer until ready to use.

WINE PAIRING: MAISON VEVEY ALBERT BLANC DE MORGEX ET DE LA SALLE

For the pasta:

2 tablespoons salt

1 pound potato gnocchi, fresh egg tagliatelle, or penne rigate

For the sauce:

½ cup whole or 2% milk

1 ¼ cups heavy cream

3 tablespoons unsalted butter

½ pound Fontina from Val d'Aosta, rind removed, coarsely grated

¾ cup (3 ounces) freshly grated Parmigiano-Reggiano or Grana Padano

⅛ teaspoon freshly grated nutmeg

½ teaspoon salt

⅛ teaspoon freshly ground black pepper

2 large egg yolks

½ cup plus 1 tablespoon finely chopped walnuts

2 tablespoons white truffle oil

Make the pasta: Bring 5 quarts of water to a boil. Add the salt and the pasta. Cook until the pasta is al dente, then drain, reserving 2 cups of the pasta cooking water.

Meanwhile, make the sauce: In a heavy-bottomed saucepan large enough to accommodate the pasta, combine the milk and the cream. Bring to a gentle boil over medium heat. Stir in the butter, and when it melts, start adding the Fontina in small handfuls while you stir constantly with a wire whisk; it is important to add the Fontina little by little, or it will curdle in the sauce. When all of the Fontina has been incorporated and is fully melted, add the

Parmigiano in small handfuls, also whisking all the while, until it also melts into the sauce. Stir in the nutmeg, salt, and pepper. (The sauce can be made up to this point 2 days in advance; refrigerate until needed, then warm gently before proceeding.) Whisk in the egg yolks, beating vigorously to prevent scrambling, and remove from the heat until you are ready to serve. You can let the sauce sit at this point for about 2 hours at room temperature. When you are ready to serve, warm very gently over low heat and stir in the walnuts; taste for seasoning and adjust as needed. Be sure to warm over low heat to prevent scorching the sauce.

To serve: Toss the drained pasta into the sauce. Sauté over low heat for 1 minute to meld the flavors, thinning out the sauce as needed with some of the reserved pasta cooking water; the texture of the sauce should be that of heavy cream. (If using gnocchi, do not sauté the gnocchi with the sauce on the stove, as they may fall apart; spoon the sauce into a large bowl and, using a rubber spatula, fold in the gnocchi and enough of the reserved pasta cooking water to thin out the sauce as needed.) Adjust the seasoning, drizzle with the truffle oil, and serve hot.

Truffles, One of Earth's Natural Aphrodisiacs

Piedmont in northern Italy is known for its *Tuber magnatum pico,* a fragrant white fungus that grows spontaneously at the base of hazelnut and oak trees, and Umbria in central Italy is renowned for its *Tuber melanosporum* Vitt., a highly aromatic black fungus that cannot be cultivated. Truffles both black and white have been sought after since antiquity, and sometimes not just for their culinary applications but for their purported aphrodisiac properties.

Slow-Cooked Savoy Cabbage Sauce with Pork

Cavolo Verza e Costine di Maiale all'Uso di Saint-Vincent Don't be put off by the lengthy cooking time; this Valdostano specialty is simplicity itself and calls for just six ingredients (butter, cabbage, pork, white wine, salt, and pepper) and very little active work. SERVES 4

Ingredient notes: Savoy cabbage is a curly green cabbage with a deeper, earthier flavor than regular cabbage; if you cannot find it, use ordinary green cabbage.

WINE PAIRING: LO TRIOLET GEWURZTRAMINER

For the sauce:

2 tablespoons (¼ stick) unsalted butter

1 head of savoy cabbage (about 1 pound), quartered, cored, and thinly sliced

1 teaspoon salt

½ teaspoon freshly ground black pepper, plus extra for serving

½ cup water, plus extra as needed

1 pound bone-in country-style pork ribs or country-style pork chops

1 cup dry white wine

For the pasta:

2 tablespoons salt

1 pound pizzoccheri (buckwheat tagliatelle), egg tagliatelle, or rigatoni

Make the sauce: In a heavy-bottomed saucepan large enough to accommodate the pasta, melt 1 tablespoon of the butter over medium heat. Add the cabbage, ½ teaspoon of the salt, and ¼ teaspoon of the pepper. Stir and cook for about 5 minutes, until the cabbage browns a bit around the edges and takes on a smoky aroma. Pour in the water. Cover and cook over low heat until the cabbage wilts and becomes a soft, tangled mass, about 30 minutes, adding water as needed to maintain a small amount of liquid in the pan. Remove from the heat.

In a clean 12-inch sauté pan, melt the remaining tablespoon of butter over medium-high heat. Add the pork ribs in a single layer (if needed, do this in two batches to prevent crowding the pan). Brown the pork ribs on all sides for about 10 minutes, turning the ribs as needed to brown evenly. Season with the remaining ½ teaspoon of salt and ¼ teaspoon of pepper. Pour in the wine and cook for 1 minute, scraping the bottom of the pan. Bring to a gentle boil and cover. Reduce the heat to low. Simmer and cook, covered, for 1 ½ hours, or until the ribs are very tender and the meat is falling off the bone. Add water as needed to maintain about ½ cup of liquid in the pan at all times, or the meat will be dry and stringy rather than moist and delicious.

Turn off the heat. Remove the ribs to a plate, cool 10 minutes, then debone the ribs. Discard the bones and finely shred the meat or pull into chunks with your hands; stir the meat into the savoy cabbage sauce, add the pan juices from the pork, and warm through. Taste for seasoning and adjust as needed. Keep the sauce warm until ready to serve. (The sauce can be made up to this point 2 days in advance; refrigerate until needed, then warm gently before proceeding.)

Make the pasta: Bring 5 quarts of water to a boil. Add the salt and the pasta. Cook until the pasta is al dente, then drain, reserving 2 cups of the pasta cooking water.

To serve: Toss the drained pasta into the sauce. Sauté over high heat for 1 minute to meld the flavors, thinning out the sauce as needed with some of the reserved pasta cooking water. Adjust the seasoning, sprinkle with pepper, and serve hot.

Drooling Gnocchi

Head to Val d'Aosta and Piedmont, and you'll surely find *gnocchi alla bava* on local menus. Directly translated, this means "drooling gnocchi," an unappetizing description for a most delicious dish. Potato gnocchi are boiled and sauced with nothing more than melted butter (usually infused with sage) and thinly sliced Toma or Fontina cheese; the cheese melts and "drools" all over the hot gnocchi, making for a spectacularly easy and memorable presentation.

The Hunter's Rabbit Ragù

Ragù del Cacciatore Like all ragùs, this sauce takes hours to meld into an integrated whole, so plan ahead and don't rush the process. Remember to allow time for the overnight marinade. Chicken thighs are a fine substitute if you are not inclined to eat rabbit, as they do in Val d'Aosta. SERVES 4

> **Ingredient notes:** If you do not wish to search for the cloves in the ragù after cooking, use a pinch of ground cloves instead.

WINE PAIRING: CANTINA DI BARRO MAYOLET

For the marinade:

2 pounds bone-in rabbit legs or skinless bone-in
   chicken thighs
1 teaspoon salt
½ teaspoon freshly ground black pepper

½ cup red wine vinegar
2 garlic cloves, crushed
4 whole cloves (or ¹⁄₁₆ teaspoon ground cloves)
1 bay leaf

For the sauce:

2 tablespoons (¼ stick) unsalted butter
1 large yellow onion, minced (about 1 cup)
2 garlic cloves, minced
1 cup dry red wine
2 cups water, plus extra as needed
1 bay leaf

2 whole cloves (or ¹⁄₁₆ teaspoon ground cloves)
1 teaspoon salt
½ teaspoon freshly ground black pepper, plus
   extra for serving
¾ pound button mushrooms or chanterelles,
   rinsed, dried, and thinly sliced

For the pasta:

2 tablespoons salt

1 pound fresh egg tagliatelle or potato gnocchi

Make the marinade: Place the rabbit in a wide container large enough to hold the rabbit comfortably in a single layer. Rub with the salt and pepper. Pour the vinegar over the rabbit, add enough cool water to cover, and add the crushed garlic, the whole cloves, and the bay leaf. Cover and refrigerate overnight.

Drain, discarding the bay leaf, cloves, and garlic. Blot the rabbit dry with paper towels (this is very important, because if the meat is wet, it will boil rather than brown in the pan).

Make the sauce: In a heavy-bottomed saucepan large enough to accommodate the pasta, melt the butter over medium heat. Add the rabbit in a single layer (if needed, do this in two batches to prevent crowding the pan). Cook for 15 minutes, browning on all sides and turning as needed to cook evenly. Add the onion and cook for about 10 minutes, until the onion releases its aroma and becomes translucent. Stir in the garlic and cook for 2 minutes. Deglaze with the wine and cook for 1 minute, scraping the bottom of the pan. Add the water and bring to a boil. Add the bay leaf and cloves, season with the salt and pepper, and cover. Reduce the heat to low. Simmer, covered, for 1½ hours, or until the meat is tender.

Turn off the heat. Remove the rabbit to a plate, cool 10 minutes, then debone with your hands. Discard the bones and finely chop the meat with a knife, or shred the meat with your fingers; return the meat to the sauce, stir in the mushrooms, and cover. Cook over medium-low heat for 30 minutes. Add water as needed to maintain some liquid in the pan, or the meat will be dry and stringy rather than moist and delicious. Discard the bay leaf and cloves. Taste for seasoning; adjust as needed. Keep warm. (The sauce can be made up to this point 2 days in advance; refrigerate until needed, then warm gently before proceeding.)

Make the pasta: Bring 5 quarts of water to a boil. Add the salt and the pasta. Cook until the pasta is al dente, then drain, reserving 2 cups of the pasta cooking water.

To serve: Toss the drained pasta into the sauce. Sauté over high heat for 1 minute to meld the flavors, thinning out the sauce as needed with some of the reserved pasta cooking water. (If using gnocchi, do not sauté the gnocchi with the sauce on the stove, as they may fall apart; spoon the sauce into a large bowl and, using a rubber spatula, fold in the gnocchi and enough of the reserved pasta cooking water to thin out the sauce as needed.) Adjust the seasoning, sprinkle with pepper, and serve hot.

Sautéed Mushroom Sauce with Garlic, Parsley, and Cream

Sugo di Funghi Trifolati alla Panna Funghi trifolati (with garlic and parsley) are one of Italy's great side dishes; in Val d'Aosta they become a hearty sauce with the addition of a splash of cream. SERVES 4

> **Ingredient notes:** Fresh porcini are best, but they are not easy to find. Any variety of mushrooms will do; cremini, button, chanterelles, and shiitake work beautifully together. Avoid portobello mushrooms, which tend to darken sauces.

WINE PAIRING: LO TRIOLET PINOT GRIS

For the pasta:

2 tablespoons salt

1 pound fresh egg linguine, tagliatelle, or pappardelle

For the sauce:

2 tablespoons (¼ stick) unsalted butter
2 garlic cloves, minced
2 tablespoons minced fresh flat-leaf parsley
1 ½ pounds mushrooms, rinsed and thinly sliced (remove the stems if using shiitake)
1 teaspoon salt

¼ teaspoon freshly ground black pepper
1 cup dry white wine
1 cup heavy cream

½ cup (2 ounces) freshly grated Parmigiano-Reggiano or Grana Padano

Make the pasta: Bring 5 quarts of water to a boil. Add the salt and the pasta. Cook until the pasta is al dente, then drain, reserving 2 cups of the pasta cooking water.

Meanwhile, make the sauce: In a deep, wide saucepan large enough to accommodate the pasta, melt the butter over medium heat. Add the garlic and parsley and cook for about 2 minutes, until the garlic releases its aroma, watching that the garlic does not burn or take on any color. Add the mushrooms, season with the salt and pepper, and cover. Cook for about 3 minutes, or until the mushrooms begin to give up their liquid and their aroma intensifies. Cover and reduce the heat to medium-low. Cook for 5 more minutes, then add the wine and cover again; cook for 5 more minutes. Uncover, stir in the cream, and cover again. Simmer for about 5 more minutes, or until all the flavors have melded. Adjust the seasoning and keep warm. (The sauce can be made up to this point 2 days in advance; refrigerate until needed, then warm gently before proceeding.)

To serve: Transfer the drained pasta to the saucepan, add the Parmigiano, and stir to dissolve it into the sauce. Sauté over high heat for 1 minute to meld the flavors, thinning out the sauce as needed with some of the reserved pasta cooking water. Adjust the seasoning and serve hot.

Pasta al Forno, an Italian Favorite

One of the ways Italian cooks make entertaining easier is to prepare pasta al forno, or pasta in the oven, since all the active cooking can be completed ahead and all that needs to be done is baking the pasta when guests arrive. In its simplest form, boiled pasta is tossed with butter and grated cheese (whichever type is regionally or personally favored), then popped into a moderately hot oven until it becomes gloriously golden and crispy on top. Some pasta al forno recipes include chunky vegetables or ragù; some feature a rich and creamy melted cheese sauce (the ancestor of mac & cheese) or béchamel sauce. Many of the recipes in this book can be transformed into pasta al forno, and short pasta is especially well suited to oven baking. Drain the pasta when it is a minute or two shy of al dente (it will cook further in the oven), and after saucing it, transfer to a buttered or oiled roasting pan, top with grated cheese (mozzarella cheese, Fontina, Caciocavallo, or Parmigiano are all good choices), and bake at 350°F for about 30 minutes, until the top is crisp and lightly colored. Just remember that when the pasta bakes, it tends to dry out, so you'll want to be a bit more generous when saucing it.

Piedmont

Alternating between luxuriant valleys where rice and polenta grow, verdant hills where vines have thrived for centuries, and mountains where cows happily graze and Alpine lakes offer a bounty of freshwater fish, Piedmont is a rich region, both industrially and agriculturally. Named after the stunningly high mountains that define much of its northern landscape, Piedmont (literally "at the foot of the mountains") is where my family has had a home since I was a baby. Fresh and aged cow's milk cheeses, butter, milk, and cream form the basis of many pasta sauces found on the Piedmontese family table, and rich meat sauces hauntingly flavored with garlic and rosemary are a carnivore's dream. Olive oil, which was traded for wine with neighboring Liguria, has traditionally been used in many Piedmontese pasta sauces instead of butter, even though the region is too cold to plant olive trees.

Quick-Cooked Chicken and Marsala Sauce

Sugo di Pollo delle Langhe Country cooks in Piedmont make this sauce with chicken livers rather than diced boneless chicken thighs; I have adapted the sauce to my taste. What makes this dish so flavorful is the addition of garlic and rosemary toward the end of cooking. SERVES 4

Ingredient notes: Dry Marsala is best for cooking. Look for quality Sicilian Marsala (not one labeled for cooking) at a wine shop.

WINE PAIRING: CANTINE SANT'AGATA NA VOTA RUCHÈ

For the sauce:

2 tablespoons (¼ stick) unsalted butter
½ medium yellow onion, minced (about ¼ cup)
½ pound boneless and skinless chicken thighs,
   cut into ½-inch dice
1 teaspoon salt
¼ teaspoon freshly ground black pepper

1½ cups dry Marsala
¾ cup chopped San Marzano canned tomatoes
¾ cup water, plus extra as needed
2 tablespoons minced rosemary
2 garlic cloves, minced

For the pasta:

2 tablespoons salt

1 pound penne rigate, campanelle,
   or mezzi rigatoni

Make the sauce: In a deep, wide saucepan large enough to accommodate the pasta, melt the butter over medium heat. Add the onion and cook for about 2 minutes, until the onion is just soft and translucent, then stir in the chicken and cook for about 5 minutes, or until browned all over and cooked all the way through (it will no longer be pink inside when cut with a knife). Season with the salt and pepper and add the Marsala. Cook for about 5 minutes, until the Marsala almost fully evaporates, then add the tomatoes and water. Reduce the heat to medium-low, cover, and cook for 10 minutes. Stir in the rosemary and garlic and continue to cook for about 10 more minutes, or until the chicken is very tender. If needed, add ½ cup of water during the cooking to keep the sauce moist. Adjust the seasoning and keep warm. (The sauce can be made up to this point 2 days in advance; refrigerate until needed, then warm gently before proceeding.)

Make the pasta: Bring 5 quarts of water to a boil. Add the salt and the pasta. Cook until the pasta is al dente, then drain, reserving 2 cups of the pasta cooking water.

To serve: Transfer the drained pasta to the saucepan and sauté over high heat for 1 minute to meld the flavors, thinning out the sauce as needed with some of the reserved pasta cooking water. Adjust the seasoning and serve hot.

Mom's Veal Roast Sauce

I remember one evening after dinner at my parents' home, when I was growing up, my dad got up from the dinner table to get started on washing the dishes. All of a sudden my mom cried out in alarm: "Wait! Don't wash out the roasting pan from the veal. I was going to use the juices for the pasta tomorrow!" And so every time I make pasta with veal roast juices, I think of my parents and that particular evening. It is hard to give a recipe for veal roast juices . . . in fact, the accumulated juices from any roasted meat (beef, chicken, veal, pork, lamb . . . you name it) make an excellent sauce when treated correctly. The trick is this: marinate a piece of meat with garlic, rosemary, olive oil, salt, and pepper and splash with some white wine during roasting. When ready to serve, let the meat rest in the pan for 10 minutes before removing and carving. Add about 2 cups water (or chicken stock if you prefer a more intense flavor) to the drippings in the roasting pan, scrape well over high heat for about 3 minutes, or until reduced by half, strain if desired, and toss with just-drained pasta, extra-virgin olive oil or unsalted butter, and freshly grated Parmigiano.

Parmigiano Sauce with Fresh Nutmeg

Salsa Cremosa alla Biellese This sauce perfectly embodies the Piedmontese love affair with butter, cow's milk cheese, and milk. It cooks through in less time than it takes the pasta water to come to a boil. SERVES 4

Ingredient notes: Freshly grated nutmeg has a sweeter, more floral taste than pre-ground, so, if possible, buy whole nutmegs and grate just before using.

WINE PAIRING: LA SCOLCA GAVI DI GAVI BLACK LABEL

For the pasta:

2 tablespoons salt

1 pound fresh egg tagliolini or tagliatelle

For the sauce:

2 tablespoons (¼ stick) unsalted butter
¼ teaspoon freshly grated nutmeg
  (or more if desired)
1 cup whole or 2% milk

1¾ cups (7 ounces) freshly grated Parmigiano-
  Reggiano
½ teaspoon freshly ground black pepper

Make the pasta: Bring 5 quarts of water to a boil. Add the salt and the pasta. Cook until the pasta is al dente, then drain, reserving 2 cups of the pasta cooking water.

Meanwhile, make the sauce: In a deep, wide skillet large enough to accommodate the pasta, melt the butter over medium heat. Add the nutmeg and the milk and bring to a gentle simmer. Stir in half of the Parmigiano slowly, by the handful, while whisking constantly, and cook for about 3 minutes, until the Parmigiano melts and the ingredients meld into a smooth sauce. Season with the pepper and keep warm (do not let the sauce scorch; keep it on very low heat).

To serve: Transfer the drained pasta to the skillet and sauté over high heat for 1 minute to meld the flavors. Add the remaining Parmigiano little by little until it melts in, thinning out the sauce as needed with some of the reserved pasta cooking water. Adjust the seasoning and serve hot. You should be able to discern the nutmeg and the pepper, so add more if the flavors seem muted.

Crushed Hazelnut and Herb Sauce

Sugo alle Nocciole d'Alba The hilly Langhe area is known for outstanding wines, fragrant white truffles, and delectable hazelnuts. Most hazelnuts find their way into Turin's gianduja (hazelnut chocolate) and glorious hazelnut desserts, but here they are used to create an unusual savory sauce. For a vegetarian dish, simply omit the prosciutto. SERVES 4

Ingredient notes: Toasting the hazelnuts in the oven makes peeling far easier and intensifies their flavor.

WINE PAIRING: CORREGGIA ROERO RISERVA ROCHE D'AMPSEJ

For the sauce:

¼ pound hazelnuts

2 tablespoons (¼ stick) unsalted butter

8 fresh sage leaves, minced

1 tablespoon minced fresh rosemary

½ cup heavy cream

¾ teaspoon salt

½ teaspoon freshly ground black pepper

¼ pound prosciutto di Parma, in one thick slice, cut into ¼-inch dice

For the pasta:

2 tablespoons salt

1 pound fresh egg tagliatelle or spaghetti

1 large egg yolk

Make the sauce: Preheat the oven to 350°F. Spread out the hazelnuts on a rimmed baking sheet and toast in the oven for about 10 minutes, or until a shade darker. Cool, then rub with paper towels to slip off the skins. Don't worry if some bits of skin remain. Finely mince the hazelnuts (you can do this in the bowl of a food processor if you wish, but do not pulverize the nuts; there should be some texture left).

In a deep, wide saucepan large enough to accommodate the pasta, melt the butter over medium heat with the sage and rosemary. When the herbs release their aroma into the butter, after about 2 minutes, add the minced hazelnuts and the cream. Bring the cream to a gentle boil and season with the salt and pepper. Simmer for 2 minutes, adding a ladleful of water as needed to loosen the sauce if the cream evaporates. (The sauce can be made up to this point 2 days in advance; refrigerate until needed, then warm gently before proceeding.) Stir in the prosciutto and keep warm.

Make the pasta: Bring 5 quarts of water to a boil. Add the salt and the pasta. Cook until the pasta is al dente, then drain, reserving 2 cups of the pasta cooking water.

To serve: Transfer the drained pasta to the saucepan and sauté over high heat for 1 minute to meld the flavors. Add the egg yolk and stir briskly to avoid scrambling the egg, thinning out the sauce as needed with some of the reserved pasta cooking water. Adjust the seasoning and serve hot.

Anchovies in the Italian Kitchen

Anchovies are a staple in Italian cooking, especially popular in land-locked regions since they could travel from afar and conserve for long periods of time. In these areas, anchovies appear in pasta sauces, sauces for meat, antipasti, and salads: when the craving for a flavor of the sea hits, these long-keeping ingredients were used to bring a salty marine taste. In Piedmont, a luscious pasta sauce of anchovies slow-simmered with cream, butter, garlic, and olive oil is a favorite, reminiscent of the region's famed *Bagna Cauda*, a warming anchovy dip served with raw and cooked vegetables at the start of a meal. Anchovies are available salted or oil-packed; the former have a deeper, cleaner flavor, and need to be rinsed, boned, and gutted before using, which sounds like a longer process than it actually is.

Potato, Onion, and Fontina Sauce with Pancetta

Pasta Rustida della Val Vigezzo Not all pasta sauces are liquid in nature (see page xv for more on this). Here is a perfect example of such a sauce, where chunky ingredients are combined in a hot pan with some of the pasta cooking water and a generous amount of grated cheese to create a mixture that coats and flavors the pasta perfectly. SERVES 4

Ingredient notes: Look for Bra, a rich cow's milk cheese (sometimes spiked with goat's milk or sheep's milk), for a truly Piedmontese taste. Fontina from Val d'Aosta is a perfect alternative, but domestic Fontina will work well too.

WINE PAIRING: ORSOLANI LA RUSTIA ERBALUCE DI CALUSO

For the pasta:

2 tablespoons salt
½ pound Yukon Gold potatoes, peeled and cut into ½-inch dice

1 pound ditalini, conchiglie, or pizzoccheri (buckwheat tagliatelle)

For the sauce:

2 tablespoons (¼ stick) unsalted butter
1 large yellow onion, thinly sliced
¼ pound pancetta, excess fat trimmed, cut into ¼-inch dice

½ pound Fontina or Bra from Val d'Aosta, rind removed, coarsely grated
½ teaspoon salt
¼ teaspoon freshly ground black pepper

Make the pasta: Bring 5 quarts of water to a boil. Add the salt, potatoes, and pasta. Cook until the pasta is al dente and the potatoes are tender, then drain, reserving 2 cups of the pasta cooking water. (If using fresh pasta, boil the potatoes for 8 minutes prior to adding the pasta, as the pasta will cook through in 1 to 2 minutes.)

Meanwhile, make the sauce: In a deep, wide saucepan large enough to accommodate the pasta, melt the butter over medium heat. Add the onion and pancetta and cook, stirring occasionally, for about 5 minutes, or until the onion becomes translucent and the pancetta releases its fat. Reduce the heat if needed to prevent scorching. Keep the sauce warm. (The sauce can be made up to this point 2 days in advance; refrigerate until needed, then warm gently before proceeding.)

To serve: Transfer the drained pasta and potatoes to the saucepan and sauté over high heat for 1 minute to meld the flavors. Stir in the grated Bra, the salt, and the pepper, thinning out the sauce as needed with some of the reserved pasta cooking water. Adjust the seasoning and serve hot.

At the Cheese Shop

Here are a few favorite Italian cheeses available in North America:

Grana Padano: This grainy, salty, nutty-flavored cow's milk cheese from northern Italy is very similar to Parmigiano-Reggiano. Made from pasteurized milk, it can be used in any recipe that calls for Parmigiano, especially delicate cheese or creamy sauces, light meat sauces made with veal or beef, and basil pesto.

Ricotta salata: Made from sheep's milk, this is essentially salted ricotta that has been aged a few months. It is milky, salty, and slightly sweet and pairs beautifully with sauces featuring raw tomatoes, olives, capers, eggplants, or arugula.

Asiago: A firm cow's milk cheese from the Veneto that is available young and mild or aged and sharp. For oven-baked pasta dishes, young asiago provides a nice melting texture; aged asiago is ideal grated into sauces featuring nuts, veal, and radicchio.

Piave: Similar to Parmigiano-Reggiano and Grana Padano, aged piave is salty, sharp, and herbal in aroma; it is ideal with delicate meat sauces or mushroom-based sauces.

Montasio: A firm cow's milk cheese from Friuli–Venezia Giulia, montasio melts nicely when incorporated into a sauce; it mates well with salty cured meats, mushrooms, and asparagus.

Aged provolone: This cow's milk cheese, usually shaped like a pear and hung as it ages, is ideal for melting. Sharp and salty, it is wonderful with sauces featuring capers, olives, cauliflower, or pork. Smoked provolone is lovely with radicchio, endives, or fennel.

Caciocavallo: A cow's milk cheese shaped like a pear and slung over a wooden board to age, Caciocavallo melts beautifully and lends richness to sauces featuring slow-cooked tomatoes, salami, prosciutto, and other intensely flavored cured meats. It is also a great choice for oven-baked pastas.

Scamorza: Basically an aged mozzarella, it melts perfectly and is lovely atop baked pastas but also delicious in sauces featuring bitter greens, olives, fresh tomatoes, or eggplants. Smoked scamorza is especially good with radicchio or zucchini.

Mascarpone: This creamy, full-fat cow's milk cheese from Lombardy is often used in desserts (most famously tiramisù) but is also an excellent alternative to heavy cream to finish a sauce, where it provides a rich mouthfeel and buttery flavor.

Liguria

A small region shaped like a crescent, nestled between Lombardy to the north and Tuscany to the south, Liguria is home to some of Italy's most beautiful beaches and pristine mountains. Olive trees thrive on its steeply terraced hillsides; fish and seafood are abundant in its clear Mediterranean waters; porcini mushrooms, basil, artichokes, string beans, and more are plucked from its fertile soil. Whether along the coast or inland, the cooking of Liguria is restrained and subtle. This is the region that has made pesto famous all over the world. But it is not just basil pesto that often appears as a pasta sauce in these parts: there is a walnut pesto, and a marjoram and pine nut pesto too. Other pasta sauces draw on the bounty of the sea or the kitchen garden, depending on the season and the cook's inclination.

Genoese Basil Pesto

Pesto Classico Genovese Pesto alla Genovese is one of Italy's most glorious (and most ill-copied) recipes. Never warm pesto on the stovetop or it will turn unpleasantly dark and oily and lose its fresh fragrance. SERVES 4

Ingredient notes: If possible, buy (or grow) the smallest-leaved Italian basil available.

WINE PAIRING: CAMPOGRANDE CINQUETERRE BIANCO

For the pasta:

2 tablespoons salt

½ pound baby red creamer or Yukon Gold potatoes, cut into ½-inch dice

½ pound haricots verts or tender string beans, tipped

1 pound trofie, trenette, linguine, or pappardelle

For the sauce:

½ cup pine nuts

2½ cups tightly packed fresh young basil leaves (2 large bunches)

2 large, plump garlic cloves, peeled

½ teaspoon salt

½ cup extra-virgin olive oil, plus extra as needed

½ cup (2 ounces) freshly grated Parmigiano-Reggiano or Grana Padano

½ cup (2 ounces) freshly grated Pecorino Romano

Make the pasta: Bring 5 quarts of water to a boil. Add the salt and the potatoes and cook for 3 minutes. Add the haricots verts and cook for 2 more minutes. Finally, add the pasta and cook until al dente; drain, reserving 2 cups of the pasta cooking water. (You have to time the cooking of the potatoes with the beans and pasta so that all of the ingredients are perfectly cooked at the same time: if using dried pasta, which requires about 10 minutes to cook through, the timing above will work; if using fresh pasta, which cooks through in 1 to 2 minutes, give the potatoes and string beans 5 extra minutes before dropping in the pasta.)

Meanwhile, make the sauce: In the bowl of a food processor, place the pine nuts, basil, garlic, and salt. Process until finely chopped. Gradually pour in the olive oil with the motor running; the mixture will emulsify. If there is enough oil, the sauce will make a gurgling sound while the motor is running; if it looks dry or does not make a gurgling sound, add a bit more oil while the machine is running.

In a deep, wide bowl, place the pesto and stir in the Parmigiano and Pecorino. If you are not about to serve the pasta within minutes, lay plastic wrap directly on top of the pesto to prevent oxidation. (The pesto can also keep in the refrigerator 2 days, topped with a thin layer of olive oil, or, if desired, it can be frozen in ice cube trays until solid, then wrapped in plastic wrap and placed in freezer-safe bags for up to 1 month. Be sure to return the pesto to room temperature before proceeding.)

To serve: Fold ½ cup of the reserved pasta cooking water into the pesto in the bowl to loosen it. Stir in the pasta, potatoes, and haricots verts, thinning out the sauce as needed with some of the reserved pasta cooking water. Adjust the seasoning and serve hot.

Isn't That *Too Much* Salt?

As a cooking teacher, I want to be sure that my students enjoy what we cook together. But I also want them to learn that there are certain basic parameters that can't be ignored when cooking properly. One of these basic parameters is the use of salt in the kitchen. So unfortunately, I often face a student who looks on aghast as I add salt to a dish, saying (or visibly thinking), "Isn't that too much salt?" The fact is, food tastes best when it is seasoned with salt during cooking (not just when it is sprinkled with salt as an afterthought, when serving); pasta tastes better when it is boiled in properly salted water; and no dish can be made without salt if you really want to taste the ingredients to their fullest. Use good-quality sea salt (not iodized salt, which has an odd metallic flavor) and add enough salt so that each flavor in the dish aligns. And remember: when you taste a dish and you are unexcited by it, chances are that it needs more salt.

Pine Nut and Marjoram Pesto

Pesto di Pinoli e Maggiorana In Liguria, this sauce is usually paired with round, coin-shaped pasta called corzetti, which were historically prepared for weddings, stamped with celebratory motifs or the coat of arms of noble families. SERVES 4

> **Ingredient notes:** If fresh marjoram is unavailable, substitute 2 tablespoons fresh basil leaves and 1 teaspoon fresh oregano leaves instead, but don't opt for dried marjoram.

WINE PAIRING: DANILA PISANO ROSSESE DI DOLCEACQUA

For the pasta:

2 tablespoons salt

1 pound fresh egg tagliatelle or corzetti

For the sauce:

½ cup loosely packed fresh marjoram leaves (about ½ large bunch, leaves only)

2 garlic cloves, peeled

¾ cup pine nuts

½ cup whole or 2% milk, plus extra as needed

⅓ cup heavy cream

½ teaspoon salt

¼ teaspoon freshly ground black pepper

¼ cup extra-virgin olive oil

1 cup (¼ pound) freshly grated Parmigiano-Reggiano or Grana Padano

Make the pasta: Bring 5 quarts of water to a boil. Add the salt and the pasta. Cook until the pasta is al dente, then drain, reserving 2 cups of the pasta cooking water.

Meanwhile, make the sauce: In the bowl of a food processor, combine the marjoram, garlic, pine nuts, milk, cream, salt, pepper, and olive oil. Process until smooth. Add the Parmigiano and process again until smooth. If the sauce seems too thick, dilute it with additional milk. The sauce should be as thick as pesto when done. Transfer to a large bowl and set aside. (The sauce can also be refrigerated at this point for up to 2 days; return to room temperature before proceeding.)

To serve: Add ½ cup of the reserved pasta cooking water to the sauce in the bowl. Stir in the pasta, thinning out the sauce as needed with some of the reserved pasta cooking water. Adjust the seasoning and serve hot.

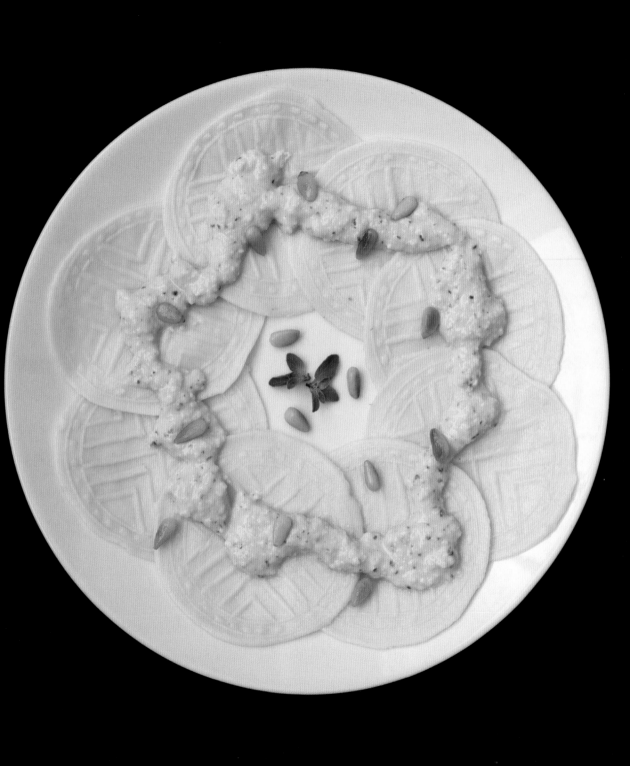

About Extra-Virgin Olive Oil

Nearly all my recipes call for extra-virgin olive oil; if I'm not using butter, I'm using extra-virgin olive oil. But why should I specify extra-virgin, rather than virgin, pure, or light olive oil, especially given that it costs so much more?

Extra-virgin olive oil is produced according to stricter guidelines than other olive oils. You need to use less in any given recipe because it delivers more flavor per tablespoon than other olive oils. The olives are picked when ripe, sent to the mill within a day of picking (so the fruit does not begin to deteriorate), and crushed mechanically. The resulting mash is spread onto thin mats that are stacked in a stainless steel press. As pressure is applied, oil and water seep out; since no heat is used, this oil is called "first cold pressed." After pressing, water and oil are separated, and the oil may or may not be filtered to remove small bits of fruit or pit. The oil is then bottled and sold as "extra-virgin olive oil."

Oils that do not meet the criteria for "extra-virgin" after pressing are sent to a refinery where defects in color, taste, and aroma are rectified by industrial processing. When olive oil is refined with the aid of chemicals, it becomes colorless and tasteless; this inferior oil is then blended with some virgin olive oil (which provides color and flavor) and sold as "pure" olive oil. "Light" and "mild" olive oils are also produced this way, using chemical processes and solvents, but less "virgin" oil is added to rectify flavor and color.

Extra-virgin olive oil is required by law to have no more than 0.8% acidity, which makes it more digestible and healthier than virgin olive oil (2% or less acidity) and pure olive oil (higher than 2% acidity). Acidity in olive oil is directly correlated to production methods: when olives are picked mechanically or bruised before they are pressed, or when the olive oil oxidizes, acidity levels increase. Therefore, lower acidity is an indication of better quality.

All olive oil (whether extra-virgin, virgin, or pure) has the same number of calories: 120 per tablespoon, so steer clear of olive oil labeled "light," which has the same calories but a much blander, nondescript flavor and higher acidity than extra-virgin olive oil.

As for most foods, heat and light are olive oil's natural enemies, causing the oil to deteriorate faster than it would otherwise, and to oxidize, eventually becoming rancid. Store olive oil away from light and heat; a pantry far from the stove is ideal. You can store olive oil in the refrigerator if you don't plan on using it within a year of purchase; the oil will turn cloudy and firm up in the refrigerator, but it will return to its liquid state when brought back to room temperature.

Olive oil oxidizes over time and will become rancid if stored for too long; the average shelf life of olive oil is eighteen months from the date of bottling, as long as it is properly stored. Some bottles have a production date stamped on the label, but most do not, so you are better off buying your olive oil at a store that has a good turnover.

If you like the flavor of extra-virgin olive oil, there is no reason to relegate it to the "raw use" category only: try extra-virgin olive oil in your pan sauces, rub it on meat before grilling, add it to marinades, deep-fry in it . . . While it is true that the characteristics of extra-virgin olive oil are more pronounced when the oil is savored raw, extra-virgin olive oil nevertheless brings more fruity olive flavor to the plate than any other oil. And it is far healthier.

Extra-virgin olive oil has a lower smoke point than chemically extracted oils, so do not heat it beyond 350°F. This is also why I start my sauces cold when using olive oil to sauté aromatic ingredients (see Starting Cold, page 32 and page xvi).

Artichoke Sauce with White Wine and Porcini Mushrooms

Sugo di Carciofi The Riviera del Ponente (to the west of Genova) is renowned for its artichokes. Sweet, tender, and small, they are often cooked with white wine, garlic, and parsley to sauce pasta. Here a handful of dried porcini mushrooms and a splash of tomato enrich the dish. SERVES 4

Ingredient notes: Look for the largest dried porcini possible; those that actually look like porcini mushrooms usually were dried from the best mushrooms.

WINE PAIRING: CANTINA CINQUETERRE COSTA DE CAMPU

For the sauce:

½ ounce dried porcini mushrooms
I lemon, halved
8 small artichokes (about 1½ pounds)
2 tablespoons extra-virgin olive oil
2 garlic cloves, minced
½ small yellow onion, minced (about 2 tablespoons)

I tablespoon minced fresh flat-leaf parsley
½ cup dry white wine
I cup Fresh Tomato Sauce (page 221) or chopped San Marzano canned tomatoes
I cup water, plus extra as needed
I teaspoon salt
⅛ teaspoon freshly ground black pepper

For the pasta:

2 tablespoons salt
I pound potato gnocchi, pappardelle, or tagliatelle

½ cup (2 ounces) freshly grated Parmigiano-Reggiano or Grana Padano

Make the sauce: Soak the porcini in a small bowl with cool water to cover for about 30 minutes, until soft. Drain (if you like, reserve the soaking water for risotto or soup), rinse thoroughly, and finely mince; set aside.

Prepare a bowl filled with water and squeeze the juice of the lemon halves into the water. Trim the artichokes, removing the tough outer leaves and the hard top portion. Rub all over with the lemon halves. Discard the stem if woody (or trim it down to its tender

(continued on page 32)

inner part if it is flexible and seems soft inside). Cut the artichokes in quarters, discard the fibrous, hairy choke inside, and then cut into thin strips. As you work, toss the strips into the bowl of water in which you have squeezed the lemon juice.

In a deep, wide saucepan large enough to accommodate the pasta, place the olive oil, garlic, onion, minced porcini, and parsley. Set over medium heat and cook for about 5 minutes, or until the onion is soft and translucent. Drain the artichoke strips and add them to the pan. Cook for 2 minutes, then add the wine and cook for about 2 more minutes, until the wine evaporates. Stir in the tomatoes, water, salt, and pepper and cover. Cook over medium-low heat for 30 minutes, adding water as needed to maintain a moist consistency to the sauce. Adjust the seasoning and keep warm. (The sauce can be made up to this point 2 days in advance; refrigerate until needed, then warm gently before proceeding.)

Make the pasta: Bring 5 quarts of water to a boil. Add the salt and the pasta. Cook until the pasta is al dente, then drain, reserving 2 cups of the pasta cooking water.

To serve: Fold the pasta into the sauce and stir in the Parmigiano. Sauté over high heat for 1 minute to meld the flavors, thinning out the sauce as needed with some of the reserved pasta cooking water. (If using gnocchi, do not sauté the gnocchi with the sauce on the stove, as they may fall apart; spoon the sauce into a large bowl and, using a rubber spatula, fold in the gnocchi and enough of the reserved pasta cooking water to thin out the sauce as needed.) Adjust the seasoning and serve hot.

Starting Cold

"Place the olive oil in a pan and add the onion, carrot, and celery. Cook over medium heat until . . ." Does this sentence seem strange or counterintuitive to you? Why would you put the ingredients together in a cold pan? Simple: starting cold brings the best out of the aromatic ingredients that form the flavor base of most Italian recipes. By gently warming these ingredients (usually finely minced, they are known as battuto in Italian) at the same time as the olive oil when preparing a sauce, you extract more of their flavor and lessen the risk of burning them. When you add aromatic ingredients to hot oil in a hot pan, you seize them and often burn them, rather than coax out their essence. The exception to the rule is butter, of course, which needs to be melted before you use it to cook or sauté.

Delicate Tomato Sauce with Diced Red Snapper

S**ugo di Dentice** This elegant sauce features celery and carrots, aromatic ingredients that are commonly used in meat ragùs (but not usually fish sauces) in northern Italy. The trick is not to cook the sauce too long. SERVES 4

Ingredient notes: In Liguria, cooks use red mullet rather than red snapper. Since red mullet is a small and bony fish, and difficult to skin and bone for this sauce, I substitute red snapper.

WINE PAIRING: TENUTA LA GHIAIA ALMAGESTO BIANCO

For the pasta:

2 tablespoons salt

1 pound spaghetti, linguine, or trenette

For the sauce:

5 tablespoons extra-virgin olive oil
1 medium yellow onion, minced (about ½ cup)
1 carrot, minced (about ½ cup)
1 celery stalk, minced (about ½ cup)
4 garlic cloves, minced
2 tablespoons minced fresh flat-leaf parsley
12 fresh basil leaves, torn
⅛ teaspoon red pepper flakes

1 pound red snapper fillets, pin bones removed, skin removed, and cut into ½-inch cubes
1 cup dry white wine
1½ cups Fresh Tomato Sauce (page 221) or chopped San Marzano canned tomatoes
1 teaspoon salt
⅛ teaspoon freshly ground black pepper

Make the pasta: Bring 5 quarts of water to a boil. Add the salt and the pasta. Cook until the pasta is al dente, then drain, reserving 2 cups of the pasta cooking water.

Meanwhile, make the sauce: In a deep, wide saucepan large enough to accommodate the pasta, place 2 tablespoons of the olive oil and the onion, carrot, celery, garlic, parsley, basil, and red pepper flakes. Set over medium heat and cook for about 5 minutes, or until the vegetables are soft and translucent. Fold in the cubed red snapper and cook, stirring often, for about 3 minutes, until the flesh turns almost white. Add the wine and cook for about 3 more minutes, until the wine nearly evaporates. Add the tomatoes, season with the salt and black pepper, and bring to a gentle boil; cover and reduce the heat to medium-low. Cook for about 10 minutes, or until the olive oil rises to the top and the sauce takes on a rich orange color. If needed, add a bit of water to the pan to prevent the sauce from drying out. Do not worry if the fish has broken up into small pieces; it will carry more of its flavor throughout the sauce that way. Adjust the seasoning and keep warm.

To serve: Fold the pasta into the sauce and sauté over high heat for 1 minute to meld the flavors, thinning out the sauce as needed with some of the reserved pasta cooking water. Adjust the seasoning, drizzle with the remaining 3 tablespoons of olive oil, and serve hot.

Fish in Ligurian Cooking

It's no surprise that a sea-hugging region such as Liguria should incorporate fish (usually the prized red mullet, or *triglia*) in its pasta sauces. Head to the fish market in any Ligurian town along the coast and you'll see an amazing array of fish and seafood varieties, plucked straight from the Mediterranean waters that very day. There are spiny scorpionfish that make full-bodied soups; delicate sea bream for roasting; sweet branzini for sautéing and grilling; a variety of slipper lobsters known as *cicale di mare,* with a flesh similar to the sweetest lobster; silvery anchovies for curing in olive oil and lemon juice; tiny briny clams and gleaming mussels best enjoyed with garlic, white wine, and parsley in a simple soup or sauté; opalescent squid, as good in long-simmered preparations as they are quickly grilled or dusted with flour and deep-fried; tuna, swordfish, sturgeon, and other large fish for grilling or smoking . . . the offerings are dizzying and form the basis of a delicate cuisine that should be sampled if you're ever in the area.

Lombardy

To most people, the name Lombardy means very little. But say Milan, and the word conjures images of sharply dressed business people and fashion runways. Milan, Lombardy's capital, is also one of Italy's most prosperous business cities. The countryside surrounding Milan is vast and prolific, and its plains are fed by the sinuous Po River, which winds its way through small medieval towns and postwar cities. In Lombardy, food is big business: Grana Padano, a nutty grating cheese similar to Parmigiano-Reggiano, is one of the country's most prized cheeses, prepared according to the same recipe since monks first made it a thousand years ago. And then there is mascarpone, and Gorgonzola, and prosciutto cotto, and farmhouse butter . . . all ingredients that find their way into many of the region's favored pasta sauces. Gnocchi, particularly those made with potatoes, are among Lombardy's most typical pastas; other common pastas are tagliatelle and tagliolini, usually made with plenty of eggs and soft wheat flour to better pair with the region's rich pasta sauces.

Slow-Cooked Cranberry Bean Sauce with Scallions, Pancetta, and Garlic-Parsley Garnish

Sugo di Fagioli alla Mantovana Pasta e fagioli, a peasant dish that usually pairs short pasta with an unctuous, long-simmered bean sauce, appears in every Italian region. Lombard cooks prefer cranberry beans (borlotti). Remember to allow time to soak the beans overnight. SERVES 4

> **Ingredient notes:** If using canned beans instead of dried beans to cut down on preparation time, drain and thoroughly rinse two 15.5-ounce cans of cranberry beans or red kidney beans.

WINE PAIRING: FRECCIAROSSA LE PRAIELLE

For the sauce:

10 ounces dried cranberry beans (use red kidney beans if cranberry beans are unavailable)

2 tablespoons (¼ stick) unsalted butter

1 medium yellow onion, thinly sliced

4 scallions (white and green parts), thinly sliced

2 garlic cloves, minced

¼ pound pancetta, finely minced

½ cup Fresh Tomato Sauce (page 221) or chopped San Marzano canned tomatoes

1½ teaspoons salt

¼ teaspoon freshly ground black pepper, plus extra for serving

For the pasta:

2 tablespoons salt

1 pound mezzi rigatoni or ditalini

2 garlic cloves, finely minced

2 tablespoons minced fresh flat-leaf parsley

Make the sauce: Soak the beans in a bowl of cool water overnight, picking out any stones and any beans that float to the top. Drain the beans. In a deep, wide saucepan large enough to accommodate the pasta, place the beans and add enough cool water to cover by 3 inches. Bring to a gentle boil over medium-low heat and simmer, covered, 1½ to 2 hours, until the beans are tender (cooking time depends on how old the beans were when you bought them; the older the beans, the longer they will take to cook through). Drain the beans and reserve 4 cups of their cooking liquid. Rinse and dry the saucepan, and place it back on the stove.

In the same saucepan, melt the butter over medium heat. Add the onion, scallions, garlic, and pancetta and cook for about 10 minutes, until the onion becomes translucent and the pancetta renders its fat. Stir in the cooked beans, 2 cups of the reserved bean cooking liquid, and the tomatoes. Season with the salt and pepper. Bring to a gentle boil and cover. Cook over medium-low heat for about 30 minutes, until the beans are very tender and the sauce has thickened nicely, stirring occasionally and adding more of the reserved bean cooking water as needed to prevent scorching. I like to crush the beans with a fork against the side of the pot while cooking so they break down into a nice, chunky purée. The consistency should be a bit soupy and thick; if the consistency is very liquid, uncover the pan and cook for 10 to 15 minutes, until the liquid reduces to your liking. Adjust the seasoning and keep warm. (The sauce can be made up to this point 2 days in advance; refrigerate until needed, then warm gently before proceeding.)

Make the pasta: Bring 5 quarts of water to a boil. Add the salt and the pasta. Cook until the pasta is almost but not quite al dente, then drain, reserving 2 cups of the pasta cooking water. The pasta will finish cooking in the sauce.

To serve: Stir the drained pasta into the sauce and sauté over medium heat for 2 minutes, stirring constantly and adding as much of the reserved bean cooking water and, when that is finished, as much of the reserved pasta cooking water as needed, until the pasta is al dente and the sauce coats the pasta well. Stir in the garlic and parsley. Adjust the seasoning, sprinkle with pepper, and serve hot.

Sage Butter, Northern Italy's Simplest Sauce

When you can take two ingredients and turn them into a sauce worthy of the most elegant dinner, you know you have something special. That's exactly the case with sage butter, northern Italy's favorite sauce for ravioli, agnolotti, tagliatelle, and even gnocchi. Simply place good-quality unsalted butter in a skillet and add plenty of fresh, just-chopped sage leaves (if you don't want to eat the sage later, keep the leaves whole and discard them after infusing them into the butter). Season with salt and pepper and warm until the butter melts and the aroma of sage suffuses the butter; you can take it a step further and brown the butter for more intensity if you wish. Toss with boiled pasta, and stretch as needed with pasta cooking water; I usually add some pasta cooking water directly to the sage butter so none of the buttery goodness stays behind in the pan. Sprinkle with freshly grated Parmigiano-Reggiano or Grana Padano and enjoy hot.

Wilted Cabbage, Potato, and Mountain Cheese Sauce

Salsa per Pizzoccheri alla Valtellinese This sauce hails from the Valtellina area at the foot of the Alps, where it is paired with pizzoccheri, fresh buckwheat noodles. SERVES 4

> **Ingredient notes:** Savoy cabbage has ruffled leaves and is tastier than regular green cabbage, but you can use regular green cabbage if savoy is unavailable.

WINE PAIRING: NINO NEGRI CA BRIONE BIANCO TERRAZZE RETICHE DI SONDRIO

For the pasta:

2 tablespoons salt

¾ pound Yukon Gold potatoes, peeled and cut into ½-inch dice

1 pound pizzoccheri (buckwheat tagliatelle) or tagliatelle

For the sauce:

2 tablespoons (¼ stick) unsalted butter

1 large yellow onion, thinly sliced

12 fresh sage leaves, thinly sliced

¾ pound savoy cabbage, quartered, cored, and thinly sliced

1 teaspoon salt

¼ teaspoon freshly ground black pepper

¼ cup water, plus extra as needed

½ cup (2 ounces) freshly grated Parmigiano-Reggiano or Grana Padano

¼ pound Raschera, Bra, or Fontina from Val d'Aosta, rind removed and coarsely grated

Make the pasta: Bring 5 quarts of water to a boil. Add the salt, potatoes, and pasta, and cook for about 10 minutes, until the potatoes are tender and the pasta is al dente. (If using fresh pasta, cook the potatoes for 8 minutes before adding the pasta to the pot.) Drain, reserving 2 cups of the pasta cooking water.

Meanwhile, make the sauce: In a deep 2-quart saucepan, melt the butter over medium heat. Add the onion and sage and cook for about 5 minutes, until the onion is translucent and just starting to caramelize. Stir in the cabbage. Season with the salt and pepper, add the water, cover, and cook, stirring occasionally, for about 10 minutes, until the cabbage is limp and lightly browned in spots, adding a bit of water by the spoonful as needed to prevent the cabbage from burning or drying out. There should always be about ¼ cup of liquid in the pan. Taste the cabbage for salt and pepper, adjust the seasoning, and keep warm. (The sauce can be made up to this point 2 days in advance; refrigerate until needed, then warm gently before proceeding.)

To serve: Transfer the pasta to a deep serving bowl. Stir in the sautéed cabbage and onion and ½ cup of the reserved pasta cooking water. Sprinkle with the Parmigiano first, then with the Raschera, thinning out the sauce as needed with some of the reserved pasta cooking water. Adjust the seasoning and serve hot.

Buckwheat Pasta, One of Northern Italy's Most Beguiling Specialties

We may associate buckwheat noodles with Japan's famous soba noodles, but in Italy's northern regions—especially Lombardy—buckwheat pasta has long been a staple. In Lombardy's Valtellina, a series of green valleys bordering Switzerland, cooks prepare handmade buckwheat pasta called *pizzocheri*. Very delicate in texture, because buckwheat flour has no gluten, these dark, nutty-flavored noodles are most often paired with Swiss chard in the summer months or cabbage in the winter. Some wheat flour and eggs are added to the buckwheat flour to ensure that the dough holds together, but the flavor of the buckwheat flour shines through and gives the pasta a distinctive sweetness. Buckwheat flour is also used along with cornmeal in the Valtellina to make a hearty polenta known as *polenta taragna*, streaked with melting Fontina or the local Bitto cheese and served piping hot on cool days.

Mom's Beef Ragù

I Ragù della Mamma Here is my mom's ragù: ground beef, onions, carrots, celery, a hint of tomato, and a bit of patience. Unlike most other ragùs, this one does not call for mincing the aromatic vegetables: rather, the aromatic vegetables are coarsely chopped so you get a textural surprise and a bit more sweetness in some bites. SERVES 4

Ingredient notes: Ask the butcher for beef chuck that is 80% lean and 20% fat. Avoid sirloin or other lean ground beef, as it will result in ragù with a gummy texture.

WINE PAIRING: CASTELLO DI STEFANAGO CROATINA ROSSO DI PAVIA

For the sauce:

2 tablespoons extra-virgin olive oil

1 medium yellow onion, cut into ½-inch pieces (about ½ cup)

1 carrot, cut into ½-inch pieces (about ½ cup)

1 celery stalk, cut into ½-inch pieces (about ½ cup)

1 pound ground beef chuck (80% lean)

1 teaspoon salt

¼ teaspoon freshly ground black pepper

2 garlic cloves, minced

20 fresh basil leaves, torn

1 cup chopped San Marzano canned tomatoes

1½ cups water, plus extra as needed

1 bay leaf

For the pasta:

2 tablespoons salt

1 pound potato gnocchi, penne rigate, or mezzi rigatoni

½ cup (2 ounces) freshly grated Parmigiano-Reggiano or Grana Padano, plus extra for passing at the table

2 tablespoons (¼ stick) unsalted butter

Make the sauce: In a deep, wide saucepan large enough to accommodate the pasta, place the olive oil, onion, carrot, and celery and cook over medium heat for about 10 minutes, until the onion, carrot, and celery become soft.

Add the beef and cook, stirring often to break up the meat, for about 5 minutes, until the beef loses its pink color. Continue to cook for 5 to 10 more minutes, until the beef takes on a deep golden-brown color and any liquid in the pan evaporates, watching that the beef does not burn. (The browning step is crucial to developing good flavor in any ragù; if you rush this step, your ragù will taste bland rather than rich.) Add the salt and pepper and stir in the garlic and basil. Stir and cook for about 2 more minutes, or until the garlic and basil give some of their aroma to the sauce. Stir in the tomatoes and water. Drop in the bay leaf and make sure it is fully submerged in the liquid. Cover and cook over low heat for 2 hours, adding a bit of water as needed to prevent scorching and to keep the sauce pleasantly moist. Adjust the seasoning and keep warm. (The sauce can be made up to this point 2 days in advance; refrigerate until needed, then warm gently before proceeding.)

Make the pasta: Bring 5 quarts of water to a boil. Add the salt and the pasta. Cook until the pasta is al dente, then drain, reserving 2 cups of the pasta cooking water.

To serve: Fold the pasta into the warm sauce in the saucepan and stir in the Parmigiano. Sauté over high heat for 1 minute to meld the flavors, thinning out the sauce as needed with some of the reserved pasta cooking water. Remove from the heat and stir in the butter, letting it melt. (If using gnocchi, do not sauté the gnocchi with the sauce on the stove, as they may fall apart; spoon the sauce into a large bowl and, using a rubber spatula, fold in the gnocchi and enough of the reserved pasta cooking water to thin out the sauce as needed.) Discard the bay leaf, adjust the seasoning, and serve hot. Pass around more Parmigiano, to sprinkle on top.

Saving Parmigiano Cheese Rinds

There is nothing quite like the richness of flavor that a rind of Parmigiano cheese lends a simmering ragù, a bubbling soup pot, or a simmering bean stew. I buy my Parmigiano in wedges, not only because its flavor is better, but because I can be certain that I am getting an authentic product from Emilia-Romagna: the rind is stamped with the consortium's seal, ensuring me that I am paying for the real thing. When I get the cheese home, I grate it as needed, and reserve the rind to drop into simmering ragùs. By the time the ragù is ready, the rind will be soft and malleable, and can be plucked out before serving; much of its flavor will have infused into the sauce, giving it a wonderful richness and milky fragrance. Some cheese shops even sell Parmigiano rinds for a fraction of the cost of the cheese itself.

Mom's Creamy Gorgonzola Sauce

La Salsa al Gorgonzola della Mamma When I was a child, my mother often made this delicious dish. She sometimes tossed the sauce with rigatoni or penne and baked the pasta until the top got crispy and brown. SERVES 4

> **Ingredient notes:** Gorgonzola is a rich, blue-veined cow's milk cheese from Lombardy. It melts beautifully and can be creamy (known as Dolcelatte, aged just 2 months) or sharp (known as Piccante, aged three months or more). The Dolcelatte will yield a milder, less assertive sauce.

WINE PAIRING: CASTELLO DI STEFANAGO RIESLING "SAN ROCCO"

For the pasta:

2 tablespoons salt

1 pound potato gnocchi or rigatoni

For the sauce:

1 cup (¼ pound) imported Dolcelatte Gorgonzola, crusts removed and cheese crumbled

3 tablespoons heavy cream

1 tablespoon unsalted butter

½ cup (2 ounces) freshly grated Parmigiano-Reggiano or Grana Padano

¼ teaspoon freshly ground black pepper, plus extra for serving

Make the pasta: Bring 5 quarts of water to a boil. Add the salt and the pasta. Cook until the pasta is al dente. Drain and place in a large bowl, reserving 2 cups of the pasta cooking water.

Meanwhile, make the sauce: In a 1-quart pot, place the Gorgonzola, cream, butter, Parmigiano, and pepper. Set over medium-low heat. Cook gently, stirring constantly with a wooden spoon to avoid lumps. Bring to a simmer and cook for about 5 minutes, until creamy and smooth. Keep warm on a very low heat. (The sauce can be made up to this point 1 week ahead and refrigerated, then warmed gently before proceeding.)

To serve: Using a rubber spatula, fold the warm sauce into the drained pasta (be careful if using gnocchi, as they are very delicate), thinning out the sauce as needed with some of the reserved pasta cooking water. Adjust the seasoning, sprinkle with pepper, and serve hot.

Trentino–Alto Adige

Home to some of the highest mountains in all of Europe, the northern region of Trentino–Alto Adige is really two regions in one: Italian-speaking Trentino to the south, and German-speaking Alto Adige (Sud Tyrol in the past) to the north. Both areas are united by a love of butter, cream, cow's milk cheeses, and smoked pork, ingredients that are combined with cold-hardy vegetables like cabbage, beets, carrots, and potatoes to create a unique cuisine where pasta has only recently become a staple. In centuries past, soup, polenta, and potato-based first courses were the mainstays of the diet, better able to fill the belly in preparation for life in the mountains. In keeping with the historically robust nature of the cuisine, the pasta sauces of Trentino–Alto Adige are hearty and simple: spiced lightly with nutmeg or chives, embellished by pork fat or smoked pork, and rendered luscious by cream and butter.

Hunter-Style Sauce with Mushrooms and Smoked Prosciutto

Sugo alla Cacciatora The mountains of Trentino–Alto Adige are full of mushrooms, and locals often go foraging on weekends. The mushrooms find their way into sauces for pasta, meat, or fish; some are simply cooked with parsley and garlic to create a savory side dish. This sauce makes the most of mushrooms, speck (smoked prosciutto), and cream. SERVES 4

Ingredient notes: Use a combination of mushrooms for the best flavor: cremini, chanterelles, fresh shiitake, morels, and oyster mushrooms all work. Avoid portobello mushrooms though; they would give a very dark color to the sauce.

WINE PAIRING: ABBAZIA DI NOVACELLA PRAEPOSITUS LAGREIN RISERVA

For the pasta:

2 tablespoons salt

1 pound spaghetti, tagliatelle, or cheese ravioli

For the sauce:

2 tablespoons (¼ stick) unsalted butter
1 medium yellow onion, thinly sliced
½ pound mushrooms, rinsed, trimmed, and thinly sliced
¾ teaspoon salt
½ teaspoon freshly ground black pepper, plus extra to serve

½ cup heavy cream

¼ pound thinly sliced speck, cut into ⅛-inch-wide strips
½ cup (2 ounces) freshly grated Parmigiano-Reggiano or Grana Padano

Make the pasta: Bring 5 quarts of water to a boil. Add the salt and the pasta. Cook until the pasta is al dente, then drain, reserving 2 cups of the pasta cooking water.

Meanwhile, make the sauce: In a deep, wide saucepan large enough to accommodate the pasta, melt the butter over medium-low heat. Add the onion and mushrooms and season with the salt and pepper. Stir well. Cover and cook for about 10 minutes, stirring occasionally, until the onion is soft and the mushrooms have given up some of their liquid; if the mushrooms stick to the pan, add a bit of water to prevent scorching and cover again. Pour in the cream. Cover again and cook for about another 5 minutes, just long enough to warm through. Adjust the seasoning and keep warm. (The sauce can be made up to this point 2 days in advance; refrigerate until needed, then warm gently before proceeding.)

To serve: Transfer the drained pasta to the saucepan, stir in the speck and Parmigiano, and sauté over high heat for 1 minute to meld the flavors, thinning out the sauce as needed with some of the reserved pasta cooking water. Adjust the seasoning, sprinkle with pepper, and serve hot.

Smoked Pork Sauce with Chives

Salsa all'Erba Cipollina con Maiale Affumicato The family larder in Trentino–Alto Adige is rarely without smoked pork. German butchers carry smoked pork loin or smoked pork chops; both will work as long as they are deboned. SERVES 4

Ingredient notes: If chives are unavailable, use fresh flat-leaf parsley and thinly sliced scallion greens.

WINE PAIRING: KOFERERHOF KERNER ALTO ADIGE VALLE ISARCO

For the pasta:

2 tablespoons salt

1 pound fresh egg pappardelle or potato gnocchi

For the sauce:

2 large egg yolks

1 cup heavy cream

½ cup snipped fresh chives

½ teaspoon salt

½ teaspoon freshly ground black pepper, plus extra for serving

2 tablespoons (¼ stick) unsalted butter

½ teaspoon ground caraway seeds

½ pound smoked pork loin, cut into ¼-inch pieces

½ cup (2 ounces) freshly grated Parmigiano-Reggiano

Make the pasta: Bring 5 quarts of water to a boil. Add the salt and the pasta. Cook until the pasta is al dente, then drain, reserving 2 cups of the pasta cooking water.

Meanwhile, make the sauce: In a bowl, whisk the egg yolks, cream, chives, salt, and pepper.

In a deep, wide saucepan large enough to accommodate the pasta, melt the butter over medium heat. Add the caraway seeds and pork; cook for about 5 minutes, until the pork is golden. Keep warm.

To serve: Transfer the drained pasta to the saucepan and sauté over high heat for 1 minute to meld the flavors. Add the egg yolk mixture; stir to prevent the egg yolks from scrambling. Stir in the Parmigiano and pepper, thinning out as needed with some of the reserved pasta cooking water. (If using gnocchi, do not sauté the gnocchi with the sauce on the stove, as they may fall apart; spoon the sauce into a large bowl and, using a rubber spatula, fold in the gnocchi and enough of the reserved pasta cooking water to thin out the sauce as needed.) Adjust the seasoning and serve hot.

Sweet Pastas in Italy

Sweet pasta dishes, especially gnocchi and lasagna, are commonplace throughout Italy; many recipes call for sprinkling boiled pasta with sugar and cinnamon, ricotta cheese and sugar, or crushed sweetened walnuts; in Friuli–Venezia Giulia, fresh egg noodles are often tossed with a sweet paste of poppy seeds and sugar cooked in butter.

Creamy Tomato Sauce with Speck, Nutmeg, and Basil

Sugo Rosato con Speck, Noce Moscata e Basilico This sauce will take you about 10 minutes to pull together; the addition of freshly grated nutmeg brings an unexpected fragrance to the dish. SERVES 4

Ingredient notes: Speck is a smoked prosciutto from Trentino–Alto Adige. If you cannot find it, use a combination of prosciutto di Parma and bacon, adding the bacon to the pan along with the onion and mushrooms, and the prosciutto toward the end of the cooking.

WINE PAIRING: I VIGNETI VERNATSCH

For the pasta:

2 tablespoons salt

1 pound potato gnocchi, tagliatelle, or lasagne ricce

For the sauce:

2 tablespoons (¼ stick) unsalted butter
2 garlic cloves, minced
1 dried chili pepper
1 cup Fresh Tomato Sauce (page 221) or chopped San Marzano canned tomatoes
⅔ cup heavy cream
12 fresh basil leaves, cut into thin strips or torn

3 ounces thinly sliced speck, cut into ¼-inch-wide strips
½ teaspoon salt
½ teaspoon freshly ground black pepper
⅛ teaspoon freshly grated nutmeg

½ cup (2 ounces) freshly grated Parmigiano-Reggiano or Grana Padano
12 fresh basil leaves, cut into thin strips or torn

Make the pasta: Bring 5 quarts of water to a boil. Add the salt and the pasta. Cook until the pasta is al dente, then drain, reserving 2 cups of the pasta cooking water.

Meanwhile, make the sauce: In a deep, wide saucepan large enough to accommodate the pasta, melt the butter over medium heat. Add the garlic and chili pepper and cook for about 30 seconds, until the garlic is aromatic but not dark in color; discard the chili pepper. Add the tomatoes and cream and bring to a gentle boil. Stir in the basil, speck, salt, pepper, and nutmeg. Cover and simmer over medium-low heat for about 10 minutes, or until the sauce has taken on a delicate rosy hue and the aromas of speck and basil have permeated the sauce. Adjust the seasoning and keep warm. (The sauce can be made up to this point 2 days in advance; refrigerate until needed, then warm gently before proceeding.)

To serve: Transfer the drained pasta to the saucepan and stir in the Parmigiano and basil. Sauté over high heat for 1 minute to meld the flavors, thinning out the sauce as needed with some of the reserved pasta cooking water. (If using gnocchi, do not sauté the gnocchi with the sauce on the stove, as they may fall apart; spoon the sauce into a large bowl and, using a rubber spatula, fold in the gnocchi and enough of the reserved pasta cooking water to thin out the sauce as needed.) Adjust the seasoning and serve hot.

Cooking with Wine

Beware of cooking wine. Seasoned with salt, made from inferior grapes, it is not good enough for drinking—so it isn't good enough for cooking. Whatever the characteristics of a wine, they will be amplified during the cooking process; so if it starts off astringent and salty, it will become even more so after it hits the pan. Simply use whatever you have left from last night's dinner for cooking, or use some of the wine you plan to serve with the meal. The general rule is that if a wine would pair nicely with a dish, it would also be good cooked in the dish itself.

Brandied Pork and Mushroom Sauce

Sugo alla Castellana Cubes of pork tenderloin are sautéed with onion, garlic, and mushrooms, deglazed with brandy, and finished with a splash of cream, resulting in an elegant sauce. The trick is not to overcook the pork: as soon as the pork is no longer pink, add the brandy and then the cream. SERVES 4

Ingredient notes: If you are a fan of grappa, use it instead of the brandy to deglaze the pan, as they often do in Trentino.

WINE PAIRING: EUGENIO ROSI VALLAGARINA POIEMA

For the pasta:

2 tablespoons salt

1 pound potato gnocchi or fresh egg tagliatelle

For the sauce:

2 tablespoons (¼ stick) unsalted butter

1 medium yellow onion, minced (about ½ cup)

3 garlic cloves, minced

½ pound mushrooms, rinsed, trimmed, and cut into ¼-inch dice

½ pound pork tenderloin, trimmed of all fat and sinew, cut into ¼-inch dice

3 ounces thickly sliced speck, cut into ¼-inch dice

1 teaspoon salt

½ teaspoon freshly ground black pepper, plus extra for serving

½ cup brandy or grappa

1 cup heavy cream

Make the pasta: Bring 5 quarts of water to a boil. Add the salt and the pasta. Cook until the pasta is al dente, then drain, reserving 2 cups of the pasta cooking water.

Meanwhile, make the sauce: In a deep, wide saucepan large enough to accommodate the pasta, melt the butter over medium heat. When the butter is foaming, add the onion and garlic and cook for about 3 minutes, or until the onion is just golden. Stir in the mushrooms and cook, stirring often, for about 5 minutes, or until the mushrooms have given up all of their liquid and are lightly browned in spots. Stir in the pork and speck. Season with the salt and pepper. Cook, stirring constantly, for about 2 minutes, until the pork loses its raw pink color, then pour in the brandy; be careful, as the brandy may ignite, so stand back from the pan and have a lid handy in case you need to smother the flames. Cook for about 2 minutes, or until the brandy evaporates, then add the cream and bring to a gentle boil. Adjust the seasoning and keep warm.

To serve: Transfer the drained pasta to the saucepan and sauté over high heat for 1 minute to meld the flavors, thinning out the sauce as needed with some of the reserved pasta cooking water. (If using gnocchi, do not sauté the gnocchi with the sauce on the stove, as they may fall apart; spoon the sauce into a large bowl and, using a rubber spatula, fold in the gnocchi and enough of the reserved pasta cooking water to thin out the sauce as needed.) Adjust the seasoning, sprinkle with pepper, and serve hot.

Friuli–Venezia Giulia

Bordered by Austria to the north and Slovenia to the east, Friuli–Venezia Giulia bears the imprint of its neighbors (and past rulers) in its cuisine. Polenta, soups, and rice dishes are more commonly served at the family table than pasta, but when pasta does make an appearance, it is usually freshly made, often stuffed with cheese, meat, or mountain greens, and sauced with hearty concoctions. There are flavor combinations found nowhere else in Italy: dill, paprika, tarragon, cloves, cinnamon, and cocoa make their way into savory dishes, and a penchant for sweet mingled with savory hints at Austro-Hungarian and Slavic rule. In the mountains, smoked prosciutto and farmhouse cheeses lend deep flavor to pasta sauces; in the hills, where grapevines thrive, wine is used to provide sultry depth to slow-simmered ragùs for pasta; and along the coastline, seafood and fish star in many pasta dishes.

Slow-Cooked Beef Cheek Ragù

Ragù di Guancia di Manzo e Vino Rosso alla Friulana The tricky thing about braising beef cheeks is that they need to cook longer than you might think; even after 2 hours, they may still be rubbery, in which case they need to cook longer. The test of doneness is when a fork can cut a piece in half without any effort. SERVES 4

Ingredient notes: Beef cheeks can be difficult to find but are worth seeking out at Italian and specialty butchers. Veal cheeks can be used instead; they are more expensive and leaner. For best texture, trim the fat and sinew off the beef cheeks before dicing them.

WINE PAIRING: CANTARUTTI SCHIOPPETTINO

For the sauce:

1 tablespoon unsalted butter
3 tablespoons extra-virgin olive oil
1 medium yellow onion, minced (about ½ cup)
1 carrot, minced (about ½ cup)
1 celery stalk, minced (about ½ cup)
1 pound trimmed, defatted beef cheeks, cut into ½-inch pieces
¼ cup unbleached all-purpose flour

1 teaspoon salt
½ teaspoon freshly ground black pepper, plus extra to serve
1 cup dry red wine
1 cup water, plus extra as needed
1 teaspoon tomato paste
2 tablespoons minced rosemary

For the pasta:

2 tablespoons salt
1 pound mezzi rigatoni or pennette

1 cup (¼ pound) freshly grated Parmigiano-Reggiano or Grana Padano

Make the sauce: In a deep, wide saucepan large enough to accommodate the pasta, warm the butter and 1 tablespoon of the olive oil over medium heat. Add the onion, carrot, and celery, and cook for about 5 minutes, or until soft. In a large bowl, toss the beef cheeks with the flour. Add the beef cheeks to the pan, along with any flour that is coating the meat, and cook, stirring occasionally, for about 10 minutes, until the meat is browned all over. Season with the salt and pepper. Add the wine and scrape the bottom of the pan to release any bits of flour or caramelized vegetables. Stir in the water and the tomato paste, cover, reduce the heat to medium-low, and cook for about 2 hours, adding water as needed, until the beef cheeks are very tender; they should be so tender that you can easily shred them with a fork. Stir in the rosemary and continue to cook, covered, for another 15 minutes, to mingle the flavors. Adjust the seasoning and keep warm. (The sauce can be made up to this point 2 days in advance; refrigerate until needed, then warm gently before proceeding.)

Make the pasta: Bring 5 quarts of water to a boil. Add the salt and the pasta. Cook until the pasta is al dente, then drain, reserving 2 cups of the pasta cooking water.

To serve: Transfer the drained pasta to the saucepan. Stir in the remaining 2 tablespoons of olive oil and the Parmigiano and sauté over high heat for 1 minute to meld the flavors, thinning out the sauce as needed with some of the reserved pasta cooking water. Adjust the seasoning, sprinkle with pepper, and serve hot.

Knowing When Meat Is "Tender"

One of the things I've noticed after teaching cooking for so many years is that a lot of people have trouble gauging when braised meats are tender. Braising meat is the preferred method for cooking tough cuts such as shoulder, butt, and other muscles that work hard and need long, slow cooking with plenty of liquid to become tender. Most people undercook braised meats, stopping shy of when the meat magically changes texture and becomes silky and tremulous at the touch of a fork. To test whether meat is truly tender, poke it with a fork; if there is resistance, you're not there yet. Keep going, and you'll find that eventually the meat falls off the bone (if it is being cooked on the bone) or flakes when the tines of the fork penetrate it. Be sure to keep the meat nicely moistened with liquid as you braise it, or it will emerge dry and tough no matter how long you cook it.

Preserving Fresh Herbs

Fresh herbs are always in abundant supply in my refrigerator, both at home and at my cooking school. I find that with the exception of bay leaves and oregano, dried herbs really don't add much to a dish. Their flavor is usually dull and dusty, just a ghost of the lovely fragrance of the fresh herb. A lot of people are hesitant about buying fresh herbs because they figure they won't be able to use them up before they wilt or get soggy. Here is how to conserve fresh herbs when you simply have too much on your hands. Start by rinsing the herbs, then dry them thoroughly by laying them out on paper towels. At this point, you have several choices:

1. Wrap in clean, dry paper towels and wrap in a new freezer-safe plastic bag in the least cold part of your refrigerator for a few days; this works for all but the most delicate herbs (basil is notably prone to go dark and soggy after a day or so, and cannot be rinsed more than 30 minutes or so in advance of use).

2. Strip the herbs from the stems, and place in a food processor with an equivalent volume of coarse sea salt; pulse until you obtain a fine salt. This herbed sea salt can be stored in a clean glass jar in the refrigerator for a few months, but will lose potency over time. Use herbed salt in place of salt in any dish. Sturdy herbs such as rosemary, thyme, and sage do especially well in this preparation, because their aroma lasts longer.

3. Strip the herbs from the stems, place in a blender or food processor with a bit of sea salt, and add enough extra-virgin olive oil while the motor is running to create an emulsion. This herbed olive oil will last in the refrigerator for a week or so, losing potency over time. Top with a fresh layer of olive oil as needed.

4. Strip the herbs from the stems, and chop coarsely. Place in ice cube trays, cover with extra-virgin olive oil, and freeze until solid. Pop out of the ice cube trays, wrap in plastic, and store in freezer-safe plastic bags for up to 2 months. Defrost as needed. Delicious melted on a grilled steak or grilled fish, or swirled into a simmering pasta sauce upon serving!

Salami Sauce Quick-Stewed in White Wine

Sugo Rapido di Salame al Vino Bianco This easy sauce capitalizes on just-made salami, the sort Friulian families hung in their cellar for a month or so after the yearly pig slaughter in January. Look for a soft salami (it should be almost squeezable); if all the salami you find is firm, substitute sweet Italian sausage out of its casings. SERVES 4

> **Ingredient notes:** Montasio is a firm, grateable cow's milk cheese; if you cannot find it, substitute aged Piave cheese or aged Asiago cheese; even Parmigiano-Reggiano or Grana Padano will work.

WINE PAIRING: STURM RIBOLLA GIALLA

For the pasta:

2 tablespoons salt	1 pound cheese tortelloni, rigatoni, or penne rigate

For the sauce:

2 tablespoons unsalted butter	¼ teaspoon salt
½ pound fresh, soft Italian salami, peeled and cut into ¼-inch dice	½ teaspoon freshly ground black pepper
2 cups dry white wine	½ cup (2 ounces) freshly grated Montasio cheese

Make the pasta: Bring 5 quarts of water to a boil. Add the salt and the pasta. Cook until the pasta is al dente, then drain, reserving 2 cups of the pasta cooking water.

Meanwhile, make the sauce: In a deep, wide saucepan large enough to accommodate the pasta, melt 1 tablespoon of the butter over medium-low heat. Add the salami and cook for about 2 minutes, or until the fat starts to seep out. Add the wine; scrape the bottom of the pan to dislodge any bits that may have stuck. Cook, uncovered, for about 10 minutes, until the wine almost evaporates, then season with the salt and pepper; there should still be about ⅓ cup of wine in the pan when you are done cooking the salami. Keep warm.

To serve: Transfer the drained pasta to the saucepan, stir in the remaining tablespoon of butter and the Montasio, and sauté over high heat for 1 minute, thinning out as needed with some of the reserved pasta cooking water. Adjust the seasoning; serve hot.

Warm Poppy Seed Butter with Smoked Ricotta

Burro ai Semi di Papavero con Formaggio Affumicato This recipe bears the imprint of Austro-Hungarian rule on the cuisine of Friuli–Venezia Giulia. I especially love the combination of poppy seeds with smoked ricotta cheese and a sprinkling of sugar. Sugar on pasta may sound odd, but it really does work in this sauce. SERVES 4

Ingredient notes: If smoked ricotta cheese is unavailable, use a combination of smoked mozzarella cheese and ricotta salata cheese.

WINE PAIRING: BORC DODON SCODAVACCA VERDUZZO

For the pasta:

2 tablespoons salt

1 pound fresh egg tagliatelle or reginette

For the sauce:

½ cup poppy seeds

4 tablespoons (½ stick) unsalted butter

1½ cups (6 ounces) freshly grated smoked ricotta cheese, or ¾ cup (3 ounces) freshly grated

smoked mozzarella cheese and ¾ cup (3 ounces) freshly grated ricotta salata cheese

Salt and freshly ground pepper to taste

2 tablespoons sugar (optional)

Make the pasta: Bring 5 quarts of water to a boil. Add the salt and the pasta. Cook until the pasta is al dente, then drain, reserving 2 cups of the pasta cooking water.

Meanwhile, make the sauce: In a spice grinder or the bowl of a small food processor, grind the poppy seeds to a powdery paste; they will still be visibly grainy but finer than whole. In a saucepan large enough to accommodate the pasta, warm the butter over medium heat. Add the poppy seeds and warm through, cooking for about 2 minutes, until aromatic, making sure not to brown the butter. Keep warm on the lowest heat.

To serve: Transfer the drained pasta to the saucepan and sauté with the poppy seed butter over medium heat for 1 minute to meld the flavors, thinning out as needed with some of the reserved pasta cooking water. Sprinkle with the smoked ricotta and stir well. If necessary, add salt and pepper to taste, sprinkle with the sugar if you like, and serve hot.

Grouper Sauce with Olives, Aromatic Herbs, and Tomatoes

S ugo di Cernia con Olive, Erbe Aromatiche e Pomodoro The curious (and delicious) thing about this Friulian sauce is the way the grouper is flaked after it simmers with the tomatoes, olives, and herbs, permeating the sauce with its delicate flavor (for photograph see page iv). SERVES 4

Ingredient notes: If grouper is not available, red snapper or Mediterranean sea bass (branzino) will work well too.

WINE PAIRING: BRESSAN PIGNOL

For the sauce:

1 pound ripe, juicy tomatoes, cored

¼ cup extra-virgin olive oil

2 garlic cloves, minced

3 tablespoons minced fresh flat-leaf parsley

16 fresh basil leaves, torn

1 pound grouper fillets, bones and skin removed

¼ cup pitted black olives, chopped

1 teaspoon salt

½ teaspoon freshly ground black pepper

For the pasta:

2 tablespoons salt

1 pound pennette or spaghetti

Make the sauce: Bring 1 quart of water to a boil. Have a large bowl of cool water handy by the pot of boiling water. Using a paring knife, cut an X into the bottom of each tomato. Drop the tomatoes into the boiling water; cook for about 30 seconds for ripe tomatoes and about 2 minutes for firmer tomatoes, until the skins begin to loosen. Drain the tomatoes. Place them in the bowl of cool water for 5 minutes, then drain them and slip off the skins. Cut the tomatoes in half crosswise and scoop out the seeds. Finely dice the tomatoes and set aside; collect any of the juices from the cutting board and add them to the diced tomatoes.

In a deep, wide saucepan large enough to accommodate the pasta, place 2 tablespoons of the olive oil. Add the garlic, parsley, and basil, then arrange the grouper fillets over the herbs. Cook over medium heat for about 2 minutes, until the grouper starts to give off its aroma, then add the olives, tomatoes, salt, and pepper. Turn the grouper fillets in the sauce and cover the pan with a lid. Reduce the heat to medium-low and cook for about 10 minutes, or until the grouper is fully cooked and the tomatoes have broken down to a nice, chunky sauce. Add water as needed to keep the sauce moist. Flake the grouper using a large spoon. Adjust the seasoning and keep warm.

Make the pasta: Bring 5 quarts of water to a boil. Add the salt and the pasta. Cook until the pasta is al dente, then drain, reserving 2 cups of the pasta cooking water.

To serve: Stir the drained pasta into the sauce and sauté over medium heat for 1 minute to meld the flavors, thinning out the sauce as needed with some of the reserved pasta cooking water. Stir in the remaining 2 tablespoons of olive oil. Adjust the seasoning and serve hot.

The Veneto

Mention the Veneto, and most of us think of Venice: sinuous canals, dramatic gondolas, romantic alleys, golden palazzi . . . But Venice is only part of the beauty of this varied region. Bordered by Austria to the north, the Veneto boasts snowcapped mountains, gentle hills, and a stunning coastline along the Adriatic Sea. While polenta and rice form the basis of the region's cuisine, fresh pasta nonetheless plays an important role, and it is sauced with whatever the land and the sea offer up: squab, geese, aged cheese, and salty prosciutto inland, and fresh sardines, scallops, crab, cuttlefish, squid, and scampi along the sea. A touch of cinnamon and cloves typically lends a haunting flavor to ragùs, a legacy of the Venetian spice trade that made the region a superpower in the Middle Ages. The region's famed radicchio is a frequent partner for fresh pastas, as are slow-cooked anchovies cooked to melting tenderness with plenty of olive oil and onions.

Venetian-Style Two-Meat Ragù

Ragù di Piccione e Maiale al Vino Bianco Squab is much loved in the Veneto, frequently cooked into succulent sauces for pasta; pairing it with pork, as in this recipe, offsets its gaminess. SERVES 4

> **Ingredient notes:** Squab is available from most reputable butchers, but it may need to be special-ordered; most butchers will debone the squab if asked. Use boneless and skinless chicken thighs if squab is hard to find, but avoid chicken breast, as it is too lean.

WINE PAIRING: VALDADIGE TERRA DEI FORTI ENANTIO

For the sauce:

2 tablespoons extra-virgin olive oil

1 small yellow onion, minced (about ¼ cup)

1 celery stalk with leaves on, minced (about ½ cup)

¾ pound boneless and skinless squab, cut into ½-inch dice

¼ pound ground pork shoulder

2 garlic cloves, minced

1 teaspoon minced rosemary

2 cups dry white wine

1 cup Fresh Tomato Sauce (page 221) or chopped San Marzano canned tomatoes

1½ cups water, plus extra as needed

1 teaspoon salt

½ teaspoon freshly ground black pepper, plus extra for serving

1 bay leaf

For the pasta:

2 tablespoons salt

1 pound penne rigate or reginette

1 cup (¼ pound) freshly grated Parmigiano-Reggiano or Grana Padano

Make the sauce: In a deep, wide saucepan large enough to accommodate the pasta, place the olive oil, onion, and celery. Cook over medium heat for about 5 minutes, until the onion and celery are translucent. Add the diced squab and pork. Cook, stirring often to crumble the pork, for about 10 minutes, or until the pork is browned all over. Add the garlic and rosemary and cook for about 2 minutes, or until aromatic. Add the wine and scrape the bottom of the pan to dislodge any of the caramelized bits that may have stuck. After about 3 minutes, when the wine almost fully evaporates, add the tomatoes, water, salt, and pepper. Bring to a gentle boil and drop in the bay leaf, fully submerging it in the liquid so that it infuses more effectively into the sauce. Cover and cook over medium-low heat for about 1 hour, or until the flavors have melded and the meat is very tender, adding water as needed to keep the sauce moist. Adjust the seasoning and keep warm. (The sauce can be made up to this point 2 days in advance; refrigerate until needed, then warm gently before proceeding.)

Make the pasta: Bring 5 quarts of water to a boil. Add the salt and the pasta. Cook until the pasta is al dente, then drain, reserving 2 cups of the pasta cooking water.

To serve: Transfer the drained pasta to the saucepan and stir in the Parmigiano. Sauté over high heat for 1 minute to meld the flavors, thinning out the sauce as needed with some of the reserved pasta cooking water. Adjust the seasoning, sprinkle with pepper, and serve hot.

Great Finishes

Most of us think about cheese when we imagine sprinkling something over a finished pasta dish . . . yet there are many other ways to finish a pasta and give it an additional layer of flavor just before serving. For pretty much any pasta sauce that incorporates olive oil, I like drizzling my finished pasta with raw olive oil; the raw oil has incredible flavor and fruitiness compared to oil that has been warmed or cooked, so I often use less olive oil to cook a sauce, and drizzle the rest over the pasta when serving. I also love the crunch and nutty flavor provided by toasted bread crumbs; this is a classic way to finish pastas in southern Italy and Sicily (see pages 175 and 211). For seafood sauces and long-simmered bean sauces, I find a little bit of finely minced garlic and parsley add a lovely freshness. Almost any pasta tossed with a tomato-based sauce benefits from a few torn basil leaves; and there are few pasta sauces, especially those rich with cheese and slow-cooked meat, that aren't improved by a last-minute sprinkling of black pepper.

Crab Sauce with Saffron and Brandy

Sugo al Granchio con Brandy, Zafferano e Panna Spider crab is a favorite along the Adriatic Coast, and in fact the Venetians are famous for their crab risotto and pasta with crab. A splash of brandy and cream makes this sauce elegant enough for entertaining, but the preparation is straightforward. SERVES 4

> **Ingredient notes:** If you like scallops, substitute 1 pound of bay scallops for the crab; add the scallops after the shallots become translucent, before deglazing with the brandy.

WINE PAIRING: FILIPPI TURBIANA TREBBIANO

For the pasta:

2 tablespoons salt

1 pound fresh tagliatelle or pappardelle

For the sauce:

2 tablespoons (¼ stick) unsalted butter
2 large shallots, minced (about ⅔ cup)
2 garlic cloves, minced
2 tablespoons minced fresh flat-leaf parsley
⅓ cup brandy

1 cup heavy cream
¼ teaspoon saffron threads
1 teaspoon salt
¼ teaspoon freshly ground black pepper
1 pound jumbo lump crabmeat, picked over

Make the pasta: Bring 5 quarts of water to a boil. Add the salt and the pasta. Cook until the pasta is al dente, then drain, reserving 2 cups of the pasta cooking water.

Meanwhile, make the sauce: In a deep saucepan large enough to accommodate the pasta, melt the butter over medium heat. Add the shallots, garlic, and parsley and cook for about 5 minutes, until the shallots are translucent. Deglaze the pan with the brandy; cook for 1 minute. The brandy may ignite, so stand back and have a lid handy. Stir in the cream and bring to a boil. Crumble in the saffron; cook for about 3 minutes, until golden and thick enough to coat the back of a spoon. Season with the salt and pepper. Stir in the crab, being careful to leave it whole. Adjust the seasoning and keep warm.

To serve: Stir the pasta into the sauce. Sauté over high heat for 1 minute, thinning out as needed with some of the reserved pasta cooking water. Adjust the seasoning and serve hot.

Sweet Pea and Pancetta Sauce for the Feast of San Zeno

Sugo di Bisi per la Festa di San Zeno San Zeno is the patron saint of Verona, and every year in May, Verona's citizens honor their protector with concerts and parades and by cooking a springtime pasta with peas, onions, and pancetta. **SERVES 4**

> **Ingredient notes:** Most people assume fresh peas are better than frozen. Not always: as they sit for a day or longer in the refrigerator at the market, the sugars in the peas convert to starch. If you aren't shucking your own fresh peas, opt for frozen petite peas.

WINE PAIRING: CONTRA SOARDA MARZEMINO NERO GAGGION

For the sauce:

1 spring onion or 6 scallions (white part only)
2 ounces thinly sliced pancetta
12 sprigs of fresh flat-leaf parsley
2 tablespoons extra-virgin olive oil

½ pound (2 cups) frozen petite peas, thawed, or fresh shucked peas
1 teaspoon salt
½ teaspoon freshly ground black pepper
1 cup whole or 2% milk, plus more if needed

For the pasta:

2 tablespoons salt
1 pound fresh egg linguine or tagliatelle

1 cup (¼ pound) freshly grated Parmigiano-Reggiano or Grana Padano

Make the sauce: On a cutting board, finely mince the spring onion with the pancetta and parsley. In a deep, wide saucepan large enough to accommodate the pasta, place the olive oil and the pancetta-onion mixture. Cook over medium heat, stirring occasionally, for about 5 minutes, or until the ingredients release their aroma and the pancetta has rendered its fat. Add the peas, season with the salt and pepper, and then add the milk. Reduce the heat to medium-low and cover. Cook for about 20 minutes, or until the peas are tender, adding water (or more milk if you prefer) as needed to keep the peas moist; there should always be about ½ cup of liquid in the pan. Fresh peas may take as long as 30 minutes to soften.

Adjust the seasoning and keep warm. (The sauce can be made up to this point 2 days in advance; refrigerate until needed, then warm gently before proceeding.)

Make the pasta: Bring 5 quarts of water to a boil. Add the salt and the pasta. Cook until the pasta is al dente, then drain, reserving 2 cups of the pasta cooking water.

To serve: Transfer the drained pasta to the saucepan and stir in the Parmigiano. Sauté over high heat for 1 minute to meld the flavors, thinning out the sauce as needed with some of the reserved pasta cooking water. Adjust the seasoning and serve hot.

Caramelized Radicchio and Onion Sauce

Sugo al Radicchio Rosso all'Uso di Verona Slow-cooking radicchio tames its bitterness, as does adding plenty of onions and a bit of pancetta. SERVES 4

Ingredient notes: Radicchio (either the round Chioggia or the elongated Treviso variety) is typical in Veneto's cuisine. Endive makes a fine (if less colorful) substitute.

WINE PAIRING: CA' RUGATE STUDIO BIANCO

For the sauce:

2 tablespoons extra-virgin olive oil
2 garlic cloves, minced
1 large yellow onion, minced (about 1 cup)
3 ounces pancetta, minced

1 pound radicchio (about 2 large or 3 medium heads), quartered, cored, and cut into thin strips
1 ¼ teaspoons salt
½ teaspoon freshly ground black pepper
1 cup water, plus extra as needed

For the pasta:

2 tablespoons salt
1 pound penne candele, rigatoni, or penne rigate

1 cup (¼ pound) freshly grated Parmigiano-Reggiano or Grana Padano

Make the sauce: In a deep, wide saucepan large enough to accommodate the pasta, place the olive oil, garlic, and onion. Cook over medium heat for 10 minutes, until the onion caramelizes. Add the pancetta and cook for 2 more minutes, or until it releases its fat and takes on a golden color. Add the radicchio, salt, and pepper, and stir. Cook for 5 minutes, uncovered, then add the water, reduce the heat to medium-low, and cover. Cook for 30 minutes, or until tender, adding water as needed to keep the radicchio moist; there should always be about ½ cup of liquid in the pan. Adjust the seasoning; keep warm. (The sauce can be made up to this point 2 days in advance; refrigerate until needed, then warm gently before proceeding.)

Make the pasta: Bring 5 quarts of water to a boil. Add the salt and the pasta. Cook until the pasta is al dente, then drain, reserving 2 cups of the pasta cooking water.

To serve: Transfer the pasta to the saucepan; stir in the Parmigiano. Sauté over high heat for 1 minute, thinning out as needed with some of the reserved pasta cooking water. Adjust the seasoning; serve hot.

Emilia-Romagna

Often referred to as "Italy's Food Basket," Emilia-Romagna is the birthplace of many of Italy's most glorious food products: prosciutto di Parma, mortadella, Parmigiano-Reggiano, balsamic vinegar from Modena, culatello, and more. Large-scale agriculture and food production are at the core of the region's prosperity, and the cuisine here reflects the abundance of the land. In the golden valleys and plains of Emilia, the cooking is especially rich, and cream, butter, and meat are used with great abandon; in the mountains and along the coast of Romagna, there is a bit more restraint in the kitchen, and the cooking is simpler, often relying not on butter and cheese but rather on vegetables and olive oil to lend flavor to preparations. But in both Emilia and Romagna, pasta reigns supreme, and some of the local pasta sauces have become iconic of Italian cuisine the world over.

Classic Bolognese Ragù

Ragù **Classico alla Bolognese** The ragù made in Bologna is renowned internationally, but it is frequently misrepresented and poorly made outside its native city. A true Bolognese ragù features veal, pork, beef, and pancetta. Very little tomato is used, and the liquid is either stock or milk, or both. I like using both because the proteins in the milk render the meat exquisitely tender.

SERVES 4

> **Ingredient notes:** The meats for a ragù Bolognese are classically minced with a knife. You can ask your butcher for coarsely ground meat instead, to make preparation easier. Don't use sirloin or lean ground beef: this ragù needs a fatty cut like chuck.

WINE PAIRING: LA STOPPA MACCHIONA

For the sauce:

4 tablespoons (½ stick) unsalted butter
¼ pound pancetta, minced
1 medium yellow onion, minced (about ½ cup)
1 carrot, minced (about ½ cup)
1 celery stalk, minced (about ½ cup)
10 ounces pork shoulder or butt, cut into ⅛-inch cubes

7 ounces beef chuck (at least 80% fat), cut into ⅛-inch cubes
3 ounces veal shoulder, cut into ⅛-inch cubes
1 cup dry red wine
1 cup beef or chicken stock, or water
¼ cup tomato paste
1½ teaspoons salt
¼ teaspoon freshly ground black pepper
2 cups whole or 2% milk, plus extra as needed

For the pasta:

2 tablespoons salt
1 pound garganelli, fresh spinach, or egg tagliatelle

1 cup (¼ pound) freshly grated Parmigiano-Reggiano or Grana Padano

Make the sauce: In a heavy, deep saucepan large enough to accommodate the pasta, melt 2 tablespoons of the butter over medium heat. Add the pancetta, onion, carrot, and celery and cook for about 15 minutes, stirring often. The vegetables should soften but not color.

Add the pork, beef, and veal and cook, stirring occasionally, for about 15 minutes. The meat should brown and take on a rich, golden color. Avoid stirring too often at this stage, or the meat will not brown. If the meat is not sufficiently browned, the ragù will taste flat, so do not rush the browning step.

Deglaze with the wine and cook for about 10 minutes, until the wine almost fully evaporates. Add the stock and tomato paste, season with the salt and pepper, and cook for about 5 minutes, until the stock is almost completely absorbed.

Pour in the milk and cover the pan; reduce the heat to low and simmer gently for about 2 hours, or until the milk has been absorbed, the meats are very tender, and the ragù is aromatic. If the ragù dries out, add more milk as needed; there should always be about ½ cup of liquid in the pan to keep the meat moist. Adjust the seasoning and keep warm. (The sauce can be made up to this point 2 days in advance; refrigerate until needed, then warm gently before proceeding.)

Make the pasta: Bring 5 quarts of water to a boil. Add the salt and the pasta. Cook until the pasta is al dente, then drain, reserving 2 cups of the pasta cooking water.

To serve: Transfer the drained pasta to the saucepan and stir in the Parmigiano. Sauté over high heat for 1 minute to meld the flavors, thinning out the sauce as needed with some of the reserved pasta cooking water. Stir in the remaining 2 tablespoons of butter, adjust the seasoning, and serve hot.

Romagna-Style Ragù with Marsala and Crispy Prosciutto

Ragù **alla Romagnola** Like ragù Bolognese, Romagna's ragù is deeply aromatic, but it is less rich. It differs from its Bolognese cousin in that veal alone is used, more tomato is added, and Marsala provides moisture (rather than dry red wine and milk) after the meat is browned. SERVES 4

Ingredient notes: The meat for this ragù is typically minced with a knife, but you can ask your butcher to coarsely grind the veal instead to cut down on preparation time.

WINE PAIRING: LUSENTI BONARDA LA PICCIONA

For the sauce:

2 tablespoons (¼ stick) plus 1 teaspoon unsalted butter
1 medium yellow onion, minced (about ½ cup)
1 carrot, minced (about ½ cup)
1 celery stalk, minced (about ½ cup)
2 tablespoons minced fresh flat-leaf parsley
½ pound veal shoulder, cut into ⅛-inch cubes
1 cup dry Marsala
1 cup beef or chicken stock, plus extra as needed

2 cups Fresh Tomato Sauce (page 221) or chopped San Marzano canned tomatoes
1 teaspoon salt
¼ teaspoon freshly ground black pepper
⅛ teaspoon ground cinnamon
⅛ teaspoon freshly grated nutmeg
¼ pound prosciutto di Parma in one thick slice, cut into ¼-inch cubes

For the pasta:

2 tablespoons salt
1 pound garganelli, mezzi rigatoni, or penne rigate

1 cup (¼ pound) freshly grated Parmigiano-Reggiano or Grana Padano

Make the sauce: In a heavy, deep saucepan large enough to accommodate the pasta, melt 2 tablespoons of the butter over medium heat. Add the onion, carrot, celery, and parsley and cook, stirring often, for about 15 minutes. The vegetables should soften but not color.

Add the veal and cook for about 15 minutes, stirring occasionally. The meat should brown and take on a rich, golden color. Avoid stirring too often at this stage, or the meat will not brown. If the meat is not sufficiently browned, the ragù will taste flat, so do not rush the browning step.

Deglaze with the Marsala and cook for about 10 minutes, until the wine almost fully evaporates. Add the stock and tomatoes, season with the salt and pepper, and stir in the cinnamon and nutmeg. Reduce the heat to medium-low and simmer gently for about 2 hours, or until the ragù is tender and aromatic. If the ragù dries out, add more stock as needed. Adjust the seasoning and keep warm. (The sauce can be made up to this point 2 days in advance; refrigerate until needed, then warm gently before proceeding.)

Meanwhile, in a small skillet, melt the remaining teaspoon of butter over medium heat. Add the prosciutto cubes and sauté for about 3 minutes, until the prosciutto is lightly crisp around the edges. Set aside.

Make the pasta: Bring 5 quarts of water to a boil. Add the salt and the pasta. Cook until the pasta is al dente, then drain, reserving 2 cups of the pasta cooking water.

To serve: Transfer the drained pasta to the saucepan and stir in the Parmigiano. Sauté over high heat for 1 minute to meld the flavors, thinning out the sauce as needed with some of the reserved pasta cooking water. Adjust the seasoning and serve hot, topped with the crispy prosciutto.

Prosciutto di Parma and Parmigiano Sauce

Sugo al Prosciutto di Parma Saltato Nothing could be simpler than this sauce from Parma, which highlights two of the city's most beloved ingredients. To wow your guests, serve it tableside in a hollowed-out wheel of Parmigiano. SERVES 4

Ingredient notes: Prosciutto di Parma is widely available; if possible, buy the real thing, and not a domestic version. And to be sure you are getting real Parmigiano-Reggiano, buy it in a block and check the rind: it should bear the consortium's distinctive stamp.

WINE PAIRING: CA DE NOCI BIANCO NOTTEDILUNA

For the pasta:

2 tablespoons salt

1 pound fresh tagliatelle or pappardelle

For the sauce:

5 ounces thickly sliced prosciutto di Parma (about 3 slices), fat trimmed and reserved

3 tablespoons unsalted butter

½ small yellow onion, minced (2 tablespoons)

½ teaspoon freshly ground black pepper

1 cup (¼ pound) freshly grated Parmigiano-Reggiano

Make the pasta: Bring 5 quarts of water to a boil. Add the salt and the pasta. Cook until the pasta is al dente, then drain, reserving 2 cups of the pasta cooking water.

Meanwhile, make the sauce: Cut the lean part of the prosciutto into ¼-inch dice and finely mince the reserved fat.

In a heavy, deep saucepan large enough to accommodate the pasta, melt the prosciutto fat and the butter over medium heat. Add the onion; cook for 5 minutes, or until golden. Add the lean diced prosciutto and cook for 5 minutes, until just warm and starting to crisp around the edges. Season with the pepper and remove to a bowl; do not rinse out the pan but remove it from the heat.

To serve: Transfer the pasta to the saucepan; stir in the Parmigiano by the handful while sautéing over medium heat for 1 minute, thinning out as needed with some of the reserved pasta cooking water. Adjust the seasoning; serve hot, topped with the prosciutto.

Slow-Cooked Sausage Ragù with Milk and a Hint of Tomatoes

Sugo di Salsiccia al Latte This savory ragù from Emilia makes the most of a few farmhouse staples: onions, pork sausage, milk, tomatoes, and wine. It is the slow, gentle cooking that draws out the best from each of these ingredients; in classic Emilian style, milk is used to tenderize the meat as it simmers. SERVES 4

Ingredient notes: Look for imported Italian tomato paste (often labeled tomato concentrate when made in Italy) for the sweetest flavor; I buy mine in a tube, and I check the label to make sure that it contains only tomatoes and salt.

WINE PAIRING: ZERBINA ALBANA DI ROMAGNA SECCO AS

For the sauce:

1 tablespoon extra-virgin olive oil
1 large yellow onion, minced (about 1 cup)
1 pound sweet Italian sausages, casings removed and sausages crumbled
1 cup dry white wine

1 cup whole or 2% milk
1 tablespoon tomato paste
½ teaspoon salt
¼ teaspoon freshly ground black pepper

For the pasta:

2 tablespoons salt
1 pound garganelli, penne rigate, or rigatoni

1 cup (¼ pound) freshly grated Parmigiano-Reggiano or Grana Padano

Make the sauce: In a wide heavy saucepan large enough to accommodate the pasta, place the olive oil and the onion. Cook over medium heat for about 10 minutes, until the onion softens and takes on a golden color, being careful not to brown it too much. Add the crumbled sausage to the pan and cook for about 10 minutes, stirring often and breaking up the sausage into small bits, until it is nicely browned all over. Add the wine and cook for about 2 minutes, until it nearly evaporates, scraping the bottom of the pan to dislodge any bits that may have stuck. Stir in the milk and the tomato paste and season with the salt and pepper. Bring to a boil and cover; reduce the heat to medium-low and cook for 1½ hours, adding water as needed to keep the sauce moist. Adjust the seasoning and keep the sauce warm. (The sauce can be made up to this point 2 days in advance; refrigerate until needed, then warm gently before proceeding.)

Make the pasta: Bring 5 quarts of water to a boil. Add the salt and the pasta. Cook until the pasta is al dente, then drain, reserving 2 cups of the pasta cooking water.

To serve: Add the pasta to the sauce and stir in the Parmigiano. Sauté over high heat for 1 minute to meld the flavors, thinning out the sauce as needed with some of the reserved pasta cooking water. Adjust the seasoning and serve hot.

Italian Sausage . . . Does It Even Exist?

Although my recipes habitually call for Italian sausage, the fact is, there is no such thing as Italian sausage in Italy. Every region makes many different versions of sausage. While pork is the meat most commonly used for sausage production all across Italy, the way each butcher seasons the meat, which cuts they use, how coarsely or finely ground the meat is, and the ratio of pork fat to meat all have a huge impact on the final product. In Piedmont, there are sausages flavored with cabbage or moistened with cooked rice; in Abruzzo and Molise, liver is often added; in the Veneto, horsemeat is used, and in Tuscany, wild boar is the star of many sausages; in Umbria, black truffles provide deep flavor, while in Emilia-Romagna, nutmeg lends sweetness; the list goes on and on. When I refer to Italian sausage in my recipes, I am referring to the sort of sausage typical of southern Italy: lightly flavored with garlic and black pepper, sometimes with a touch of fennel seeds or red pepper flakes for extra aroma and heat. None of these sausages, however, have preservatives or vinegar; they are made fresh by butchers, using coarsely ground pork butt or shoulder, with around 20 percent pork fat added for moistness. When buying Italian sausages, head to your local butcher instead of the supermarket, and you'll be rewarded with a tastier sausage whose flavor integrates best into your pasta sauce, with no hint of acidity. If the sausage looks very pale, rather than a nice deep orangey-pink, steer clear: it is likely chock full of fat. After all, fat is cheaper than meat, but too much fat makes for an inferior sausage, not to mention one that will clog your arteries.

Comprising the Marches, Tuscany, Umbria, and Latium, central Italy offers pastas that are quite different from those made by their northern neighbors. Here, sheep's milk cheeses (especially Pecorino Romano) reign. Heartily salted cured meats, particularly the cheek of the pig (guanciale) and rolled pig's belly (pancetta), are finely chopped into the battuto that forms the basis of many pasta sauces. And while lard was often used to cook these sauces until a few decades ago, today extra-virgin olive oil is the preferred cooking fat. Fresh ricotta cheese renders many of the area's sauces creamy without resorting to the use of heavy cream, in contrast to many of the pasta sauces of northern Italy, which are often finished with cream.

CENTRAL ITALY

The Marches

One of Italy's hidden treasures, the Marches is rarely visited by outsiders: Tuscany seems to draw most of the tourist attention in central Italy. Yet the Marches, a tranquil landscape of undulating hills, rugged woods, and glittering waters, is home to an amazing cuisine that begs to be discovered. Among its greatest offerings: pasta of all kinds. Filled and layered pastas such as ravioli, lasagne, and tortelli are commonplace on the family table, as are fresh maccheroni and tagliatelle. The small town of Campofilone in the province of Ascoli Piceno is renowned for its gossamer-thin, delicate maccheroncini, similar to northern Italy's tagliolini, made only with soft wheat flour and eggs. All this pasta means that there is a rich tradition of pasta sauces in the Marches: some are simple, like a velvety purée of potatoes; others are complex stew-like concoctions featuring all manner of fresh seafood from the Adriatic or meats from the family farm; and still others highlight the offerings of the land, like the savory vegetable sauces that adorn most everyday pastas.

Sausage and Cabbage Sauce

Sugo di Salsiccia e Cavolo Verza The combination of sausage and cabbage is thoroughly comforting. Adding a bit of tomato, as they do in the Marches, lightens the sauce and makes it equally suitable for summer or winter. SERVES 4

Ingredient notes: Fresh tomatoes are best here. Canned tomatoes are too acidic and mask the sweetness of the cabbage.

WINE PAIRING: VELENOSI LACRIMA DI MORRO D'ALBA

For the sauce:

¾ pound ripe, juicy tomatoes, cored

2 tablespoons extra-virgin olive oil

1 large yellow onion, thinly sliced

¾ pound sweet Italian sausages, casings removed and sausages crumbled

¾ pound savoy cabbage leaves, cut into ½-inch strips

1 teaspoon salt

¼ teaspoon freshly ground black pepper

For the pasta:

2 tablespoons salt

1 pound spaghetti or whole-wheat spaghetti

1 cup (¼ pound) freshly grated Parmigiano-Reggiano or Grana Padano

Make the sauce: Bring 1 quart of water to a boil. Have a large bowl of cool water handy by the pot of boiling water. Using a paring knife, cut an X into the bottom of each tomato. Drop the tomatoes into the boiling water; cook for about 30 seconds for ripe tomatoes and about 2 minutes for firmer tomatoes, until the skins begin to loosen. Drain the tomatoes. Place them in the bowl of cool water for 5 minutes, then drain them and slip off the skins. Cut the tomatoes in half crosswise and scoop out the seeds. Finely dice the tomatoes and set aside; collect any of the juices from the cutting board and add them to the diced tomatoes.

In a deep, wide saucepan large enough to accommodate the pasta, add the olive oil. Sauté the onion over medium heat for about 10 minutes, until the onion becomes translucent. Add the sausage and cook for about 10 minutes, or until nicely browned, breaking the sausage up into tiny pieces with a spoon; this will develop a good flavor base in the sauce.

Add the cabbage, season with the salt and pepper, and cover. Cook over medium-low heat for 15 minutes, stirring often and adding water as needed to prevent scorching. Add the tomatoes, bring to a gentle boil, and cover again. Cook over medium-low heat for 30 minutes, adding water as needed to keep the sauce moist. Adjust the seasoning and keep warm. (The sauce can be made up to this point 2 days in advance; refrigerate until needed, then warm gently before proceeding.)

Make the pasta: Bring 5 quarts of water to a boil. Add the salt and the pasta. Cook until the pasta is al dente, then drain, reserving 2 cups of the pasta cooking water.

To serve: Stir the drained pasta into the sauce and stir in the Parmigiano. Sauté over high heat for 1 minute to meld the flavors, thinning out the sauce as needed with some of the reserved pasta cooking water. Adjust the seasoning and serve hot.

An Elegant Pasta Presentation

Sometimes all you need to elevate a simple dish is a stunning presentation. Cacio e Pepe (Pecorino and Cracked Black Pepper Sauce, page 126) as well as any pasta featuring cheese as the sauce's primary component (such as the pasta with Parmigiano Sauce with Fresh Nutmeg on page 16 and the pasta with Prosciutto di Parma and Parmigiano Sauce on page 84) can be served in an edible cheese basket. Here's how you do it: Warm a nonstick skillet over medium heat for about 3 minutes, or until hot. Sprinkle ½ cup of Pecorino Romano, Grana Padano, or Parmigiano-Reggiano (whichever cheese is the star of your sauce) in a nice, even round in the skillet. Cook for about 3 minutes, or until melted and starting to turn golden. The cheese should form a pliable and cohesive mass; cook a little longer if needed, but watch that it does not overcook, or it will be impossible to shape into a basket later. Using a rubber spatula, lift the edge of the cheese disk and quickly remove the cheese disk from the skillet; immediately place on an inverted coffee cup or small salad bowl and let it take its shape while cooling. Remove, turn upside down, and store at room temperature in an airtight container for up to 2 days. Serve your pasta right in the cheese basket, without warming the basket first.

Shrimp Sauce with Garlic and Parsley

Sugo di Gamberetti al Prezzemolo In this Marchigiano recipe, garlic, red pepper flakes, parsley, and white wine bring out the best in shrimp. The key is to cook the shrimp just until they turn pink and are no longer opaque. SERVES 4

> **Ingredient notes:** Since this dish is best when each bite gets a bit of shrimp, I buy medium shrimp (usually labeled 31/40 per pound) and dice them after shelling and deveining.

WINE PAIRING: FATTORIA SAN LORENZO VERDICCHIO DEI CASTELLI DI JESI CLASSICO

For the pasta:

2 tablespoons salt

1 pound spaghetti, linguine, or tagliatelle

For the sauce:

¼ cup extra-virgin olive oil

2 garlic cloves, minced

⅛ teaspoon red pepper flakes

1 pound medium shrimp (31/40 per pound preferably), shelled, deveined, and tail end removed, cut into 1-inch pieces

1 cup dry white wine

1 teaspoon salt

⅛ teaspoon freshly ground black pepper

3 tablespoons minced fresh flat-leaf parsley

Make the pasta: Bring 5 quarts of water to a boil. Add the salt and the pasta. Cook until the pasta is al dente, then drain, reserving 2 cups of the pasta cooking water.

Meanwhile, make the sauce: In a deep, wide saucepan large enough to accommodate the pasta, place 2 tablespoons of the olive oil, the garlic and red pepper flakes. Cook over medium heat for 30 seconds, or until the garlic is aromatic. Raise the heat to high; add the shrimp. Sauté, stirring often, for 30 seconds. Add the wine and cook for 2 minutes, until the wine reduces by half and the shrimp are cooked, still stirring. Add the salt and black pepper, adjust the seasoning as needed, and keep warm on the lowest heat to avoid toughening the shrimp.

To serve: Fold the pasta into the sauce and sauté over high heat for 1 minute, thinning out as needed with some of the reserved pasta cooking water. Adjust the seasoning, drizzle with the remaining 2 tablespoons of olive oil, and serve hot, topped with the parsley.

Tuna, Anchovy, and Olive Sauce with Fresh Tomatoes

Sugo di Tonno con Olive, Acciughe e Pomodoro My father-in-law, Attilio, who hailed from Ascoli Piceno, made this sauce often. On hot summer days, I make the sauce without cooking it at all: I toss everything in a bowl and allow the flavors to mingle at room temperature for an hour, then stir in cooked pasta before serving, adding a bit of the pasta cooking water to thin out the sauce.

SERVES 4

Ingredient notes: Look for imported Italian or Spanish tuna in olive oil for the best flavor. Drain off the oil before stirring the tuna into the sauce, or the sauce will be greasy.

WINE PAIRING: FATTORIA VILLA LIGI PERGOLA ROSSO VERNACULUM

For the sauce:

1½ pounds ripe, juicy tomatoes, cored
2 tablespoons extra-virgin olive oil
2 garlic cloves, minced
1 tablespoon minced fresh flat-leaf parsley
2 oil-packed anchovy fillets, drained and chopped, or 1 salted anchovy, boned, gutted, and rinsed

1 7-ounce can Italian tuna packed in olive oil, drained and crumbled
⅔ cup pitted black oil-cured olives, chopped
½ teaspoon salt
¼ teaspoon freshly ground black pepper
⅛ teaspoon red pepper flakes

For the pasta:

2 tablespoons salt

1 pound spaghetti, tagliatelle, or penne rigate

Make the sauce: Bring 1 quart of water to a boil. Have a large bowl of cool water handy by the pot of boiling water. Using a paring knife, cut an X into the bottom of each tomato. Drop the tomatoes into the boiling water; cook for about 30 seconds for ripe tomatoes and about 2 minutes for firmer tomatoes, until the skins begin to loosen. Drain the tomatoes. Place them in the bowl of cool water for 5 minutes, then drain them and slip off the skins. Cut the tomatoes in half crosswise and scoop out the seeds. Finely dice the tomatoes and set aside; collect any of the juices from the cutting board and add them to the diced tomatoes.

In a deep, wide saucepan large enough to accommodate the pasta, place the olive oil. Add the garlic, parsley, and anchovies and cook over medium heat for about 2 minutes, until the anchovies break down. Stir in the tuna and olives and cook gently for 5 minutes. Add the tomatoes and season with the salt and black pepper. Stir in the red pepper flakes. Bring to a gentle boil and cook for about 10 minutes, or until the tomatoes have broken down to a nice, chunky sauce, adding water as needed to keep the sauce moist. Adjust the seasoning and keep warm.

Make the pasta: Bring 5 quarts of water to a boil. Add the salt and the pasta. Cook until the pasta is al dente, then drain, reserving 2 cups of the pasta cooking water.

To serve: Stir the drained pasta into the sauce and sauté over high heat for 1 minute to meld the flavors, thinning out the sauce as needed with some of the reserved pasta cooking water. Adjust the seasoning and serve hot.

Canned Tuna in the Italian Kitchen

Canned tuna packed in olive oil is one of the world's great convenience foods. It is never used as a substitute for fresh tuna, since its flavor and texture are so different. Rather, it is a food in its own right, used in cold salads, pasta sauces, rice dishes, and sauces for meat and poultry. In regions without access to the sea, such as Piedmont and Lombardy, canned tuna historically provided a way to enjoy a taste of the sea. Make sure you buy very good quality Italian or Spanish tuna packed in olive oil (not vegetable oil or water); the one sold in glass jars is often of superior quality. The texture of tuna packed in olive oil is richer and more buttery than tuna packed in water, and the flavor is sweeter than tuna packed in water or vegetable oil.

Smashed Potato Sauce with Cracked Black Pepper and Olive Oil

Sugo di Patate Bollite e Pepe Nero If it sounds odd to sauce pasta with boiled potatoes, as they do in the Marches, consider this: the potatoes break down as they cook along with the pasta and, when tossed with the pasta and olive oil, they form a vegetable sauce not unlike a bean purée. SERVES 4

> **Ingredient notes:** Russet (or Idaho) potatoes are too starchy to use here; Yukon Gold potatoes are perfect thanks to their sweet flavor and waxy texture.

WINE PAIRING: CLAUDIO MORELLI BIANCHELLO BORGO TORRE

For the pasta and sauce:

2 tablespoons salt

1 pound Yukon Gold potatoes, peeled and cut into ½-inch dice

1 pound spaghetti (preferably whole-wheat)

½ cup extra-virgin olive oil

½ teaspoon salt

1 teaspoon (or more to taste) freshly ground black pepper

Make the pasta and sauce: Bring 5 quarts of water to a boil. Add the salt and the potatoes; cook for about 10 minutes, until the potatoes are tender and starting to crumble a bit; the goal is to have overcooked potatoes that will easily crush when drained. Add the pasta and cook for about 10 minutes, until the pasta is al dente. (If using fresh pasta, which takes just 1 to 2 minutes to cook through, cook the potatoes for 20 minutes before adding the pasta.) Drain the potatoes and pasta, reserving 2 cups of the pasta cooking water.

To serve: In a deep serving bowl, place the olive oil, salt, and pepper. Stir in 1 cup of the pasta cooking water and mix well with a fork so the ingredients emulsify. Add the drained pasta and potatoes and toss vigorously with tongs or two forks, crushing the potatoes almost completely and creating a velvety puréed sauce; there will still be some potato chunks, which is nice and adds textural interest. Add as much of the reserved pasta cooking water as needed, until the sauce coats the pasta well. Adjust the seasoning and serve hot.

Tuscany

Tuscan cooking is like the Tuscan landscape: a thing of understated beauty. Whether they are braising meat or grilling fish, simmering pasta sauce or baking bread, Tuscans prefer a "less is more" approach. Traditional aromatics include sage, rosemary, thyme, wild mint, fennel seeds, and chili, but these are always used sparingly. Two ingredients, however, are used in abundance: olive oil (Tuscan olive trees produce an intensely flavorful oil with a pronounced fruity aftertaste) and salt (perhaps to better pair with the region's saltless bread). Sauces for pasta follow these guiding principles. The region's favorite pastas are gnocchi, ravioli, tortelli, pici, and pappardelle; depending on the season, location, and mood of the cook, these pastas are sauced with game ragùs, light veal or hearty beef sauces, wine-laced tomato sauces, fresh seafood, or simply garlic-scented toasted bread crumbs. The region's justly famous wines often find their way into many of Tuscany's flavor-charged pasta sauces, and a sprinkling of freshly grated Pecorino Toscano (Tuscan sheep's milk cheese) finishes most pastas at the table.

Silky Garlic-Tomato Sauce

Aglione I first tasted this exquisitely garlicky dish in Montepulciano; an immersion blender was used to purée the sauce, but a food processor or regular blender works well too. SERVES 4

Ingredient notes: Even though the amount of garlic seems excessive, it won't be overpowering: it becomes almost candied during the first stage of cooking and mellows further when puréed.

WINE PAIRING: AVIGNONESI ROSSO DI MONTEPULCIANO

For the sauce:

2 pounds ripe tomatoes, cored
¼ cup extra-virgin olive oil
2 heads of garlic, cloves peeled and left whole
½ small yellow onion, minced (optional)

¼ teaspoon red pepper flakes
I teaspoon salt
½ cup water

For the pasta:

2 tablespoons salt

I pound bucatini, spaghetti, or penne rigate

Make the sauce: Bring I quart of water to a boil. Have a large bowl of cool water handy by the pot of boiling water. Using a paring knife, cut an X into the bottom of each tomato. Drop the tomatoes into the boiling water; cook for about 30 seconds for ripe tomatoes and about 2 minutes for firmer tomatoes, until the skins begin to loosen. Drain the tomatoes. Place them in the bowl of cool water for 5 minutes, then drain them and slip off the skins. Cut the tomatoes in half crosswise and scoop out the seeds. Finely dice the tomatoes and set aside; collect any of the juices from the cutting board and add them to the diced tomatoes.

In a deep saucepan large enough to accommodate the pasta, place 2 tablespoons of the olive oil and the garlic, onion, and red pepper flakes. Set over medium heat and cover. Cook for about 2 minutes, or until aromatic; the garlic should not brown, or it may become acrid. Uncover and add the tomatoes and salt. Add the water, bring to a boil, cover, and cook for

10 minutes. Purée with an immersion blender until smooth, or remove to the bowl of a blender or food processor and process until smooth. Return to the saucepan and adjust the seasoning; keep warm. (The sauce can be made up to this point 2 days in advance; refrigerate until needed, then warm gently before proceeding.)

Make the pasta: Bring 5 quarts of water to a boil. Add the salt and the pasta. Cook until the pasta is al dente, then drain, reserving 2 cups of the pasta cooking water.

To serve: Sauté the pasta with the sauce over high heat for 1 minute to meld the flavors, thinning out the sauce as needed with some of the reserved pasta cooking water. Adjust the seasoning, drizzle with the remaining 2 tablespoons of olive oil, and serve hot.

All About Garlic

Invariably there is someone in my cooking classes who is surprised to see that garlic is used sparingly in my recipes. Isn't Italian cooking all about garlic? Doesn't every Italian recipe start with a lot of minced garlic? The answer is no and no. We use garlic in many recipes, of course, and there are certain regions where garlic plays a more important role (Piedmont, Abruzzo, Molise, Calabria, and Basilicata spring to mind). But the use of garlic is usually light, and garlic almost never plays center stage. For example, a true basil pesto from Liguria in northern Italy is first and foremost about the basil, then about the olive oil, and finally about the cheese; it is never about the garlic. In America, when basil pesto is made, it is often first and foremost about the garlic, then about the basil, then about the cheese, and finally about the olive oil. And in Italian cooking we almost never brown garlic in a pan before adding other ingredients because browning garlic brings out its acrid flavor; we usually start with cold olive oil if infusing garlic into a dish, then gently warm the oil with the garlic to bring out the garlic's floral aroma. Some recipes even call for discarding the garlic clove after infusing it into a sauce. Also please don't buy peeled or minced garlic; if time is short, try peeling a head or two of garlic at a time, and store the peeled cloves in an airtight container in the refrigerator for a few days. The garlic you buy peeled or minced has lost most of its fragrance and vitamins and will contribute mostly bitterness to your dish.

Fragrant Garlic and Parsley Sauce

Sugo all'Isolana Easy, exuberant, and tasty, this sauce draws on Tuscany's extra-virgin olive oil, garlic, an abundance of parsley, and Pecorino Toscano. Cooking the sauce takes less time than bringing the water to a boil, so it's ideal for busy weeknights. SERVES 4

> **Ingredient notes:** Look for Pecorino Toscano if possible; Pecorino Romano will do, but the Tuscan cheese has an aroma all its own.

WINE PAIRING: LA LASTRA VERNACCIA DI SAN GIMIGNANO

For the pasta:

2 tablespoons salt

1 pound spaghetti or pappardelle

For the sauce:

½ cup extra-virgin olive oil
6 garlic cloves, minced
¼ pound fresh flat-leaf parsley leaves, washed, dried, and minced (about 2 large bunches)
½ teaspoon salt

1 cup (¼ pound) freshly grated Pecorino Toscano or Pecorino Romano
1 teaspoon freshly ground black pepper

Make the pasta: Bring 5 quarts of water to a boil. Add the salt and the pasta. Cook until the pasta is al dente, then drain, reserving 2 cups of the pasta cooking water.

Make the sauce: In a saucepan large enough to accommodate the pasta, place the olive oil and garlic. Set over medium heat and cook for about 1 minute, or until the garlic is just aromatic; the garlic should not brown, or it may become acrid. Stir in the parsley and cook for about 2 more minutes, or until it releases its fragrance. Season with the salt and keep warm.

To serve: Sauté the pasta with the sauce, Pecorino, and pepper over high heat for 1 minute to meld the flavors, thinning out the sauce as needed with some of the reserved pasta cooking water. Adjust the seasoning and serve hot.

Wild Boar Ragù

Ragù di Cinghiale This sauce requires a bit of planning, since the boar needs to marinate overnight with red wine to tenderize it, but the cooking process is straightforward, so don't be put off by the extra step. While the sauce simmers, the aroma of rosemary is reminiscent of the Tuscan countryside, where rosemary bushes line the roads. SERVES 4

> **Ingredient notes:** Wild boar is available at specialty butchers; the shoulder cut makes the best ragù as it is marbled with fat. If you can't find wild boar at your butcher, you can make the same sauce (albeit with a less gamy flavor) with pork shoulder.

WINE PAIRING: CECCHI VINO NOBILE DI MONTEPULCIANO

For the sauce:

¾ pound trimmed wild boar shoulder, cut into 1-inch cubes

1½ teaspoons salt

2 garlic cloves, crushed

2 large sprigs of fresh rosemary

1 cup dry red wine, plus extra as needed

2 tablespoons extra-virgin olive oil

1 large yellow onion, minced (about 1 cup)

¼ pound pancetta, minced

1 tablespoon minced fresh flat-leaf parsley

1 cup chopped San Marzano canned tomatoes

½ teaspoon freshly ground black pepper, plus extra for serving

1½ cups chicken stock or water, plus extra as needed

For the pasta:

2 tablespoons salt

1 pound fresh egg pappardelle, tagliatelle, or gnocchi

Make the sauce: Place the boar in a deep container. Rub with 1 teaspoon of the salt. Add the crushed garlic cloves and the rosemary. Pour in the red wine, adding more as needed to submerge the boar, and cover with a lid. Refrigerate overnight. Drain thoroughly, reserving the marinade. Blot the boar dry with paper towels (this is very important, because if the meat is wet, it will steam rather than brown in the pan).

(continued on page 106)

In a heavy-bottomed saucepan large enough to accommodate the pasta, warm the olive oil over medium-high heat. Add the cubed boar in a single layer, along with the crushed garlic and rosemary sprigs from the marinade (if needed, brown the boar in 2 batches; if it is crowded in the pan, the boar will boil rather than brown). Brown nicely on all sides, about 15 minutes, turning as needed to cook evenly. If the boar lets out water as it cooks, keep cooking until all of the moisture evaporates and the meat starts to brown before adding the remaining ingredients.

Add the onion, pancetta, and parsley and cook for about 10 minutes, until the onion releases its aroma and becomes translucent. Deglaze with the wine from the marinade and cook, scraping the bottom of the pan, for about 5 minutes, or until the wine almost fully evaporates. Stir in the tomatoes and season with the remaining ½ teaspoon of salt and the pepper. Pour in the stock. Stir and reduce the heat to a simmer. Cook, covered, for about 1½ hours, or until the meat is tender and shreds easily when touched with a fork. Be sure that there is always about ½ cup of liquid in the pan at all times, or the meat will be dry and stringy rather than moist and delicious; add stock as needed to maintain some liquid in the pan. Discard the garlic and rosemary sprigs. Taste for seasoning and adjust as needed. Keep warm. (The sauce can be made up to this point 2 days in advance; refrigerate until needed, then warm gently before proceeding.)

Make the pasta: Bring 5 quarts of water to a boil. Add the salt and the pasta. Cook until the pasta is al dente, then drain, reserving 2 cups of the pasta cooking water.

To serve: Toss the drained pasta into the sauce. Sauté over high heat for 1 minute to meld the flavors, thinning out the sauce as needed with some of the reserved pasta cooking water. (If using gnocchi, do not sauté the gnocchi with the sauce on the stove, as they may fall apart; spoon the sauce into a large bowl and, using a rubber spatula, fold in the gnocchi and enough of the reserved pasta cooking water to thin out the sauce as needed.) Adjust the seasoning, sprinkle with pepper, and serve hot.

"False" Meat Sauce with Red Wine

Sugo Finto The Tuscan name for this sauce literally translates as "false sauce" because it is very much like a meat sauce but is completely vegetarian: aromatics are cooked down slowly, wine is added, tomatoes are stirred in, and the sauce simmers until its flavor deepens. SERVES 4

> **Ingredient notes:** Select ripe, juicy tomatoes for this sauce. Canned tomatoes (no matter how good) are too acidic and too intense.

WINE PAIRING: LA SALA CHIANTI CLASSICO RISERVA

For the sauce:

1¼ pounds ripe tomatoes, cored
¼ cup plus 2 tablespoons extra-virgin olive oil
1 large yellow onion, minced (about 1 cup)
2 carrots, minced (about 1 cup)
2 celery stalks, minced (about 1 cup)
2 garlic cloves, minced

1 tablespoon minced fresh flat-leaf parsley
½ cup dry red wine
1 cup water, plus extra as needed
1 teaspoon salt
¼ teaspoon freshly ground black pepper

For the pasta:

2 tablespoons salt
1 pound penne rigate, rigatoni, cheese ravioli, or cheese tortellini

12 fresh basil leaves, torn
½ cup (2 ounces) freshly grated Parmigiano-Reggiano or Grana Padano

Make the sauce: Bring 1 quart of water to a boil. Have a large bowl of cool water handy by the pot of boiling water. Using a paring knife, cut an X into the bottom of each tomato. Drop the tomatoes into the boiling water; cook for about 30 seconds for ripe tomatoes and about 2 minutes for firmer tomatoes, until the skins begin to loosen. Drain the tomatoes. Place them in the bowl of cool water for 5 minutes, then drain them and slip off the skins. Cut the tomatoes in half crosswise and scoop out the seeds. Finely dice the tomatoes and set aside; collect any of the juices from the cutting board and add them to the diced tomatoes.

In a saucepan large enough to accommodate the pasta, place ¼ cup of the olive oil and the onion, carrots, celery, garlic, and parsley. Set over medium-low heat and cook, uncovered, for about 10 minutes, or until very soft and aromatic. Add the wine and cook for about 3 minutes, until it evaporates. Add the diced tomatoes, water, salt, and pepper and bring to a boil. Cover and simmer for about 30 minutes; the tomatoes should break down and the sauce should take on a warm orange color. Adjust the seasoning and keep warm; add a bit of water during cooking if needed to maintain about ½ cup of liquid in the pan. (The sauce can be made up to this point 2 days in advance; refrigerate until needed, then warm gently before proceeding.)

Make the pasta: Bring 5 quarts of water to a boil. Add the salt and the pasta. Cook until the pasta is al dente, then drain, reserving 2 cups of the pasta cooking water.

To serve: Toss the pasta with the sauce. Stir in the remaining 2 tablespoons of olive oil, the basil, and the Parmigiano and sauté over medium heat for 1 minute to meld the flavors, thinning out the sauce as needed with some of the reserved pasta cooking water. Adjust the seasoning and serve hot.

Umbria

Landlocked, Umbria is one of Italy's greenest regions. In fact, Italians refer to it as "the Green Heart of Italy," a name that should hint at its verdant hills and valleys. Tiny hilltop towns crowned by castles, serene lakes, densely wooded mountains: these are the views you'll find in Umbria, a region that has only recently become a must-see on the tourist map. The cooking in this region is simple, tasty, and direct. Black truffles form an elegant sauce for pasta when slow-simmered in olive oil with anchovies and garlic; cured meat from pigs, a staple in the area, is the starting point for succulent sauces that may or may not contain tomatoes; and fresh vegetables and legumes remain the mainstay on the family table to sauce pasta, a legacy of days when meat was scarce and a handful of ingredients had to be stretched to feed hungry laborers.

Black Truffle Sauce in the Style of Spoleto

Salsa al Tartufo alla Spoletina You cannot go to Umbria without tasting this sauce. The thing to remember is to never allow the oil to warm beyond tepid.

SERVES 4

> **Ingredient notes:** The best Umbrian truffles (*Tuber melanosporum* Vitt.) are found in winter. They are black and highly aromatic, and take especially well to cooking in olive oil after being finely grated. If you cannot find fresh black truffles, use 2 tablespoons black truffle paste.

WINE PAIRING: ADANTI MONTEFALCO ROSSO RISERVA

For the pasta:

2 tablespoons salt

1 pound fresh egg linguine or stringozzi

For the sauce:

½ cup extra-virgin olive oil

1 garlic clove, crushed

4 oil-packed anchovy fillets, drained, or 2 salted anchovies, boned, gutted, and rinsed

5 ounces fresh black winter truffle (*Tuber melanosporum* Vitt.), scrubbed thoroughly with a stiff,

clean brush to get rid of soil and grit, dried, and grated on the large holes of a box grater, plus extra for serving (optional)

½ teaspoon salt

¼ teaspoon freshly ground black pepper, plus extra for serving

Make the pasta: Bring 5 quarts of water to a boil. Add the salt and the pasta. Cook until the pasta is al dente, then drain, reserving 2 cups of the pasta cooking water.

Meanwhile, make the sauce: In a heavy saucepan large enough to accommodate the pasta, place the olive oil, garlic, and anchovies. Cook over very low heat for about 5 minutes, until the anchovies break down into a purée, crushing with a fork against the bottom of the pan; do not rush this process. Discard the garlic. Add the grated truffle. Cook very gently, stirring often, for about 5 minutes, until the truffle releases its aroma and softens. Season with the salt and pepper. Keep warm. (The sauce can be made up to this point 2 hours in advance; warm gently before proceeding.)

To serve: Add the pasta to the pan. Stir in pepper; sauté over high heat for 1 minute, thinning out as needed with some of the reserved pasta cooking water. Adjust the seasoning; serve hot, garnished with truffle shavings if you like.

Egg, Sausage, and Guanciale Sauce with Lemon and Nutmeg

Sugo con Uova, Salsiccia, e Guanciale al Profumo di Limone e Noce Moscata The Umbrians have been enjoying this sauce, which is a relative of Carbonara (Roman Sauce of Eggs, Pancetta, and Parmigiano, page 121), for centuries; legend has it that a young girl first made it in the castle of Vetranola in Monteleone di Spoleto in 1494 to appease an invading army. SERVES 4

Ingredient notes: Try to buy sausage from an Italian butcher or pork shop. Avoid spicy or vinegary sausages; at the most, they should be flavored with a bit of pepper and garlic.

WINE PAIRING: ANTONELLI SAGRANTINO DI MONTEFALCO CHIUSA DI PANNONE

For the pasta:

2 tablespoons salt

1 pound linguine, rigatoni, or mezzi rigatoni

For the sauce:

1 tablespoon extra-virgin olive oil

2 ounces guanciale or pancetta, trimmed of fat and cut into ¼-inch cubes

½ pound sweet Italian sausages, casings removed and sausages crumbled

2 large eggs

2 tablespoons freshly squeezed lemon juice

¼ cup heavy cream

½ teaspoon salt

½ teaspoon freshly ground black pepper

¼ teaspoon freshly grated nutmeg

¾ cup (3 ounces) freshly grated Pecorino Romano

Make the pasta: Bring 5 quarts of water to a boil. Add the salt and the pasta. Cook until the pasta is al dente, then drain, reserving 3 cups of the pasta cooking water.

Meanwhile, make the sauce: In a heavy saucepan large enough to accommodate the pasta, place the olive oil and add the guanciale. Cook over medium heat for about 5 minutes, until the guanciale renders its fat and takes on just a little color, being careful not to brown the guanciale. Discard any fat in the pan and add the sausage. Cook, stirring often and breaking up the sausage into small pieces with a spoon, for about 8 minutes, until the sausage is fully cooked and lightly browned all over. Add 1 cup of the reserved pasta cooking water to the sausage and scrape the bottom of the pan to release any bits that have stuck to the pan and to give the sausage a nice, moist texture. Keep warm. (The sauce can be made up to this point 2 days in advance; refrigerate until needed, then warm gently before proceeding.)

Meanwhile, in a large bowl, whisk the eggs with the lemon juice, heavy cream, salt, pepper, and nutmeg. Whisk in the Pecorino.

To serve: Add the pasta to the sausage and guanciale in the pan and sauté over high heat for 1 minute to meld the flavors. Pour in the egg mixture, stirring constantly to avoid scrambling the eggs, thinning out the sauce as needed with some of the reserved pasta cooking water. Adjust the seasoning and serve hot.

Eggs in Pasta Sauces

You may find it odd that a number of pasta sauces call for beaten eggs or egg yolks to be stirred in at the end. The most famous sauce is surely Rome's *Carbonara* (Roman Sauce of Eggs, Pancetta, and Parmigiano, page 121), where the eggs take center stage; but there are many other regional pasta sauces that call for eggs. Eggs (or just egg yolks) provide great richness and creaminess without adding any milky taste; they don't dilute the other flavors in the sauce, and the fat carries other tastes and aromas very effectively. Five sauces in this book—Creamy Fontina Sauce with Crushed Walnuts and White Truffle Oil (page 3); Crushed Hazelnut and Herb Sauce (page 17); Smoked Pork Sauce with Chives (page 51); Egg, Sausage, and Guanciale Sauce with Lemon and Nutmeg (page 112); and Sautéed Zucchini, Herb, and Scallion Sauce (page 182)—owe their silky texture and richness to eggs added at the end of cooking.

Sausage, Tomato, and Asparagus Sauce

Sugo di Asparagi Selvatici In the spring, Umbrians gather wild asparagus in the fields for memorable frittate and pasta sauces. The first time I tasted this sauce was in Spoleto, and it was a revelation. SERVES 4

Ingredient notes: You can make a delicious sauce with cultivated asparagus; thinner asparagus are better than thicker for this recipe, as they should be no wider than the pasta itself. When asparagus is out of season, substitute 2 cups thawed frozen petite peas.

WINE PAIRING: ANTONELLI TREBBIANO SPOLETINO

For the sauce:

¼ cup extra-virgin olive oil
1 medium yellow onion, minced (about ½ cup)
1 carrot, minced (about ½ cup)
1 celery stalk, minced (about ½ cup)
2 garlic cloves, minced
¼ pound pancetta, finely diced
½ pound sweet Italian sausages, casings removed and sausages crumbled

2½ cups chopped San Marzano canned tomatoes
½ cup water, plus extra as needed
1 teaspoon salt
¼ teaspoon freshly ground black pepper, plus extra for serving
1 bunch of pencil-thin asparagus, woody ends trimmed, cut into 1-inch lengths (about ½ pound after trimming)

For the pasta:

2 tablespoons salt
1 pound mezzi tubetti or linguine

1 cup (¼ pound) freshly grated Pecorino Romano, plus extra for passing at the table

Make the sauce: In a heavy saucepan large enough to accommodate the pasta, place 2 tablespoons of the olive oil and the onion, carrot, celery, and garlic. Cook over medium heat for about 5 minutes, until the vegetables soften and take on a little color, being careful not to brown the vegetables too much at this point or they may burn later. Add the pancetta and crumbled sausage to the pan and cook, stirring often and breaking up the sausage into small bits, for about 10 minutes, until they are nicely browned all over. Add the tomatoes and water and season with the salt and pepper. Bring to a boil and cover; reduce the heat to

(continued on page 116)

medium-low and cook 15 minutes, adding a bit of water as needed to keep the sauce moist. (The sauce can be made up to this point 2 days in advance; refrigerate until needed, then warm gently before proceeding.) Stir in the asparagus and cover again. Cook for about 15 more minutes, or until the asparagus is quite soft. Adjust the seasoning and keep the sauce warm.

Make the pasta: Bring 5 quarts of water to a boil. Add the salt and the pasta. Cook until the pasta is al dente, then drain, reserving 2 cups of the pasta cooking water.

To serve: Add the pasta to the sauce and stir in the remaining 2 tablespoons of olive oil, the Pecorino, and pepper. Sauté over high heat for 1 minute to meld the flavors, thinning out the sauce as needed with some of the reserved pasta cooking water. Adjust the seasoning and serve hot, passing additional Pecorino at the table.

Browning Deeply for Better Flavor

Every month at our cooking school, we run a class called Fresh Pasta for Beginners, and one of the sauces we make is a beef and hot sausage ragù for our handmade tagliatelle. Invariably, as we brown the meat for the ragù, the students start to get anxious, looking at the pan in fear that we are burning the meat: they would be happy to add the wine and other liquids to the pan when the meat has barely taken on any brown color. Most people think that just cooking the meat until it loses its raw color is enough, and that taking it a good step further—until the meat caramelizes and develops a gorgeous, deep color—is equivalent to burning it and drying it out. Not so: that browning step is key to building a deep flavor base in a ragù and in any sauce that incorporates crumbled sausage. At first, the meat tends to let out liquid and boil in its own liquid, especially if it is crowded in the pan or if it had been previously frozen. Then, as the liquid evaporates and the meat starts to fry in its own fat, something magical happens: the proteins caramelize, a sweetness develops, and delicious bits stick to the bottom of the pan. . . . Next step: after the meat is nicely browned all over (the color of medium-roast coffee beans, or deep milk chocolate), it's time to deglaze; water, wine, or tomatoes can do this job, and as the bottom of the pan is scraped to release those wonderful stuck bits into the liquid, the first layer of flavor in a deeply flavored sauce is born.

Caramelized Fennel and Crumbled Sausage Sauce

Sugo di Finocchio Caramellato e Salsiccia Sbriciolata I admit that I have never eaten this pasta sauce anywhere except in our own home and at our cooking school. I developed the recipe years ago: I wanted a pasta whose flavor would capture that of a pork dish we enjoyed in Spoleto, in which a side of caramelized fennel played beautifully against a garlicky pork loin stuffed with the local sausages. SERVES 4

Ingredient notes: Pecorino Romano has the right bite to stand up to the savory sauce; Parmigiano-Reggiano or Grana Padano would be overwhelmed by the sauce's intensity.

WINE PAIRING: ROBERTO DI FILIPPO GRECHETTO SELEZIONE SASSI D'ARENARIA

For the pasta:

2 tablespoons salt

1 pound pennette or maccheroni alla chitarra

For the sauce:

¼ cup extra-virgin olive oil

1 pound sweet or hot Italian sausages, casings removed and sausages crumbled

4 garlic cloves, minced

½ teaspoon red pepper flakes

1 tablespoon fennel seeds, coarsely ground in a mortar

1 pound fennel (about 2 large bulbs), quartered, cored, and thinly sliced

½ teaspoon salt

¼ teaspoon freshly ground black pepper

1 cup water, plus extra as needed

¾ cup (3 ounces) freshly grated Pecorino Romano

Make the pasta: Bring 5 quarts of water to a boil. Add the salt and the pasta. Cook until the pasta is al dente, then drain, reserving 2 cups of the pasta cooking water.

Meanwhile, make the sauce: In a saucepan large enough to accommodate the pasta, place 2 tablespoons of the olive oil and the sausage. Cook over medium-high heat for about 10 minutes, stirring often and breaking it up into tiny pieces, until nicely browned all over.

Stir in the garlic, red pepper flakes, and fennel seeds and cook for about 30 seconds, or until just aromatic. Scatter the sliced fennel over the browned sausage and season with the salt and black pepper, then pour in the water. Stir well and scrape the bottom of the pan to release any bits of meat that may have caramelized and stuck. Cover, reduce the heat to medium, and cook, stirring occasionally, for about 8 minutes, or until the fennel has wilted down to a soft mass. There should always be about ½ cup of liquid in the pan; add water as needed to create steam for the fennel and to prevent the sausage from sticking. Adjust the seasoning and keep warm. (The sauce can be made up to this point 2 days in advance; refrigerate until needed, then warm gently before proceeding.)

To serve: Stir the drained pasta, the remaining 2 tablespoons of olive oil, and the Pecorino into the sauce in the pan. Sauté over high heat for 1 minute to meld the flavors, thinning out the sauce as needed with some of the reserved pasta cooking water. Adjust the seasoning and serve hot.

Latium

Don't be tempted to reduce Latium to its capital city, Rome: while Rome is undoubtedly a city that must be visited (possibly time and again, to better uncover its hidden beauty and quiet corners), it is in the small towns and villages of Latium that you will discover the truly pastoral character of this region. Fertile land and ancient sheepherding traditions offer Latium's cooks a vast array of ingredients to play with. Pork and lamb are favorite meats, and sheep's milk cheese and fresh ricotta cheese flavor many of the local dishes. Simple sauces for pasta combine a few well-chosen staples (perhaps black pepper and Pecorino Romano, as in Cacio e Pepe [Pecorino and Cracked Black Pepper Sauce, page 126]; or eggs, Parmigiano, and guanciale, as in Carbonara [Roman Sauce of Eggs, Pancetta, and Parmigiano, page 121]) to great effect; in fact, some of Italy's best-known pasta sauces hail from this central Italian region.

Roman Sauce of Eggs, Pancetta, and Parmigiano

Carbonara There are as many ways to prepare Carbonara as there are cooks in Rome. Some use Pecorino; others, Parmigiano; some add a peeled garlic clove or a bit of parsley. Restaurant versions call for mostly egg yolks, but I find this tastes too "eggy"; a great Carbonara is about balance among cheese, eggs, and guanciale. SERVES 4

> **Ingredient notes:** Guanciale is the cured meat from the pig's jowls. If you cannot find it, pancetta, which is salted, unsmoked pork belly, works too; bacon will also do.

WINE PAIRING: MARCO CARPINETI TUFALICCIO

For the pasta:

2 tablespoons salt

1 pound spaghetti

For the sauce:

3 large eggs
1 cup (¼ pound) freshly grated Parmigiano-Reggiano or Grana Padano
½ teaspoon freshly ground black pepper

½ pound guanciale or pancetta, fat trimmed, cut into ¼-inch dice
1 tablespoon extra-virgin olive oil
Salt as needed

Make the pasta: Bring 5 quarts of water to a boil. Add the salt and the pasta. Cook until the pasta is al dente, then drain, reserving 2 cups of the pasta cooking water.

Meanwhile, make the sauce: In a large bowl, vigorously beat the eggs with the Parmigiano and black pepper for about 2 minutes, until frothy and a bit lighter in color.

In a deep, wide saucepan large enough to accommodate the pasta, cook the guanciale and olive oil over medium heat, stirring occasionally, for 5 minutes, until the guanciale is lightly browned but not crispy. Discard any fat that the guanciale has rendered. Remove the pan from the heat.

To serve: Add the pasta to the guanciale in the saucepan and quickly pour in the egg mixture. Toss for 30 seconds using tongs, or until well combined, thinning out as needed with some of the reserved pasta cooking water. The pasta will continue to absorb liquid as it sits, so add a bit more pasta cooking water than you may think is needed. Adjust the seasoning; serve hot.

Sauces for Whole-Wheat Pasta

Students in my cooking classes often ask what sauces to pair with whole-wheat pasta. Most don't seem to be particularly excited at the prospect of eating whole-wheat pasta, but feel they should eat it since it is a healthier alternative. If you've tried whole-wheat pasta and haven't taken to it, it's probably because the sauce you paired with it was too subtle or the pasta itself was not of great quality. Since whole-wheat pasta has a stronger flavor, try it with bold, big sauces that can stand up to it: any hearty meat sauce, anchovy-based sauce, or intensely flavored vegetable sauce works. Here are a few I especially like: Slow-Cooked Savoy Cabbage Sauce with Pork (page 6); Slow-Cooked Cranberry Bean Sauce with Scallions, Pancetta, and Garlic-Parsley Garnish (page 37); Venetian-Style Two-Meat Ragù (page 69); Sausage and Cabbage Sauce (page 91); Tuna, Anchovy, and Olive Sauce with Fresh Tomatoes (page 96); Sweet Pepper and Lamb Ragù with Rosemary (page 132); Simple Lentil Sauce (page 135); and Silky Broccoli Raab, Garlic, and Crushed Red Pepper Sauce (page 179). Be sure to buy good-quality Italian whole-wheat pasta for best flavor; De Cecco and Delverde are two widely available, consistently good brands. Or try making fresh pasta at home (page 223) and substitute whole-wheat flour for half or all of the all-purpose flour.

Spicy Tomato, Onion, and Guanciale Sauce

Amatriciana If you've been to Rome, you've run across this dish. The name Amatriciana (and the sauce itself) hails from the town of Amatrice, which once belonged to neighboring Abruzzo. SERVES 4

Ingredient notes: There is no cheese better suited to Amatriciana than aged Pecorino Romano.

WINE PAIRING: CASTEL DE PAOLIS CAMPO VECCHIO ROSSO

For the pasta:

2 tablespoons salt

1 pound bucatini, spaghetti, or penne rigate

For the sauce:

¼ cup extra-virgin olive oil

1 dried chili pepper, crumbled

6 ounces guanciale or pancetta, fat trimmed, cut into ¼-inch cubes

1 large yellow onion, minced (about 1 cup)

4 garlic cloves, minced (optional but delicious)

1½ cups chopped San Marzano canned tomatoes

½ teaspoon salt

½ cup water, plus extra as needed

1 cup (¼ pound) freshly grated Pecorino Romano or Pecorino Crotonese, plus extra for passing at the table

½ teaspoon freshly ground black pepper

Make the pasta: Bring 5 quarts of water to a boil. Add the salt and the pasta. Cook until the pasta is al dente, then drain, reserving 2 cups of the pasta cooking water.

Meanwhile, make the sauce: In a heavy saucepan large enough to accommodate the pasta, place 2 tablespoons of the olive oil and the chili, guanciale, onion, and garlic. Cook over medium heat for 5 minutes, until the guanciale renders its fat. Add the tomatoes, salt, and water, bring to a boil, and cover; reduce the heat to medium-low and cook, stirring often, for 15 minutes, adding water as needed. Adjust the seasoning; keep warm. (The sauce can be made up to this point 2 days in advance; refrigerate until needed, then warm gently before proceeding.)

To serve: Add the pasta to the sauce. Stir in the remaining 2 tablespoons of olive oil, the Pecorino, and the pepper. Sauté over high heat for 1 minute, thinning out as needed with some of the reserved pasta cooking water. Adjust the seasoning; serve hot, passing Pecorino.

Pecorino and Cracked Black Pepper Sauce

Cacio e Pepe Two ingredients only, and you have an amazing dish. *Cacio* is the old Italian word for cheese, and here it must be none other than Pecorino Romano or Cacio di Roma. Grate it finely just before tossing it with the pasta. The cheese melts on contact with the hot pasta, helped along by pasta cooking water. The key to success: add the cheese to the pasta a little at a time and toss vigorously, and for longer than you may think necessary, until the pasta is creamy and well coated. SERVES 4

Ingredient notes: Tellicherry peppercorns are flavorful and widely available. Coarsely crack the pepper in a mortar with a pestle or with a mill minutes before tossing it with the pasta.

WINE PAIRING: OCCHIPINTI MONTEMAGGIORE

For the pasta:

2 tablespoons salt

1 pound spaghetti

For the sauce:

1 ¼ cups (5 ounces) Pecorino Romano or Cacio di Roma

2 teaspoons Tellicherry peppercorns

Salt as needed

Make the pasta: Bring 5 quarts of water to a boil. Add the salt and the pasta. Cook until the pasta is al dente, then drain, reserving 2 cups of the pasta cooking water.

Meanwhile, make the sauce: Finely grate the Pecorino and set aside.

Crush the peppercorns in a mortar with a pestle until cracked; they should not be pulverized, but they should not be too coarse either.

To serve: In a large bowl, place the drained spaghetti. Start adding the Pecorino and tossing vigorously with tongs to coat the pasta with the cheese. Add some of the reserved pasta cooking water and toss again. Continue in this manner, gradually adding all of the Pecorino and as much of the reserved pasta cooking water as needed to create a pasta that is well coated in sauce but not too slippery. Stir in the pepper, add salt if needed, and serve hot.

Spring Sauce of Fava Beans, Scallions, and Bacon

Sugo di Fave con Cipollotti e Pancetta Affumicata Romans cook fava beans as a side dish, stir them into soups and pasta sauces, or eat them fresh out of the pod with a wedge of Pecorino. In this recipe, they are cooked briefly with scallions, garlic, and bacon, then tossed with pasta, mint, and Pecorino for an immediate taste of spring. SERVES 4

Ingredient notes: Fresh fava beans are available at farmers' markets and Italian specialty markets in the spring. Frozen fava beans will do, but they are nowhere near as sweet and their texture tends to be mealy.

WINE PAIRING: CORTE DEI PAPI PASSERINA DEL FRUSINATE

For the sauce:

4 pounds fresh fava beans, shelled (about 3 cups shelled)

2 tablespoons extra-virgin olive oil

8 scallions (white and green parts), thinly sliced

4 garlic cloves, minced

½ pound bacon or pancetta, minced

¼ teaspoon red pepper flakes (optional)

1 cup water, plus extra as needed

1 teaspoon salt

½ teaspoon freshly ground black pepper, plus extra for serving

For the pasta:

2 tablespoons salt

1 pound fresh egg tagliolini or tagliatelle

1 cup (¼ pound) freshly grated Pecorino Romano

¼ cup fresh mint leaves, torn

Make the sauce: Bring 2 quarts of water to a boil. Add the fava beans; cook for 3 minutes, then drain. Place in a bowl of cool water and slip off the skin from each fava bean. Discard the fava bean boiling water (it may have turned quite dark from the favas, but don't be alarmed) and set the beans aside.

In a deep, wide saucepan large enough to accommodate the pasta, place the olive oil, scallions, garlic, bacon, and red pepper flakes, if using, over medium heat. Cook for about

5 minutes, or until the mixture releases its aroma and the bacon has rendered its fat. Add the water. Stir in the shelled fava beans, season with the salt and pepper, and cover. Reduce the heat to medium-low and cook for about 10 minutes, or until the fava beans are tender, adding water as needed to keep the beans moist; there should always be about 1 cup of liquid in the pan. Adjust the seasoning and keep warm. (The sauce can be made up to this point 2 days in advance; refrigerate until needed, then warm gently before proceeding.)

Make the pasta: Bring 5 quarts of water to a boil. Add the salt and the pasta. Cook until the pasta is al dente, then drain, reserving 2 cups of the pasta cooking water.

To serve: Transfer the drained pasta to the saucepan and stir in the Pecorino, mint, and pepper. Sauté over high heat for 1 minute to meld the flavors, thinning out the sauce as needed with some of the reserved pasta cooking water. Adjust the seasoning and serve hot.

Taming Strong Onions

Aside from using too much onion in a sauce, there are a few culprits that result in a sauce being too assertively oniony after cooking.

1. The onion was old. This is the case if it smells pungent when you cut into it. If the onion is old, use half the amount called for, and soak the onion in cool water to cover for 10 minutes before draining, blotting dry, and proceeding with the recipe.
2. The onion was minced improperly. The fewer cuts you make, the less of the essential oils will be liberated and the less acrid your onion will be. To properly mince an onion, cut the onion in half from root end to top end. Peel the two halves. Place one half, flat side down, on the board, and make a series of horizontal cuts parallel to the flat side of the onion, from the top end almost to the root end, but not all the way through the root end, this keeps the onion intact while slicing. Keep your hand flat on top of the onion while cutting to stabilize it. Next, make a series of vertical cuts from the top end almost all the way to the root end. Make the final cut: slice across the onion from the top end to the root end. Do not rock the knife back and forth on the small pieces you obtain, or you will release too many oils and bring out an acrid flavor in the onion.
3. The onion was not cooked long enough. When the onion has lost its raw smell, is translucent, and can easily be cut with the back of a spoon, you have cooked it long enough and can add the next ingredients to the sauce.

SOUTHERN ITALY

Six regions—Abruzzo, Molise, Apulia, Campania, Basilicata, and Calabria—make up southern Italy. In prewar years, these regions were among Italy's poorest, and they still display remarkable genius at turning a few simple, frugal ingredients into satisfying and delicious meals. Since pastas in this area are usually made without eggs (eggs were a costly ingredient until the postwar years), pasta sauces are less rich, and usually play off a single starring ingredient (such as broccoli raab, beans, mussels, or a flavorful meat) to create a symphony of flavors.

Abruzzo

Some of the best food in Italy can be found in Abruzzo. This may well be because some of the best cooks in Italy come from Abruzzo: after all, there is an exceptionally good cooking school in Villa Santa Maria. But it's not just the cooking in the restaurants and trattorie that is so memorable in this tranquil corner of southern Italy. It is the food cooked in the homes, following centuries of simple but well thought-out culinary traditions. Favorite flavorings here include spicy chili peppers, garlic, basil, parsley, bay leaves, and the locally grown saffron. Olive oil touches nearly every dish (including many sweets), and fresh sheep's and cow's milk cheeses lend depth to pasta stuffings and pasta sauces. The region's classic pasta shape is maccheroni alla chitarra, a square spaghetti cut on a stringed instrument called a *chitarra* ("guitar"), and it is tossed with every preparation imaginable: rich lamb ragùs, baby clams or mussels with white wine and garlic, basil-scented tomato sauce, or a bit of fresh ricotta cheese and some diced prosciutto.

Sweet Pepper and Lamb Ragù with Rosemary

Ragù d'Agnello e Peperoni Lamb is the favorite meat in mountainous Abruzzo, where shepherds still tend their flocks the way their ancestors did. Here, it is slow-cooked with white wine, rosemary, garlic, tomatoes, and an abundance of yellow peppers. The result is a deeply flavored sauce in which the gaminess of the lamb is offset perfectly by the sweetness of the peppers. SERVES 4

> **Ingredient notes:** Lamb ragù usually calls for very finely diced meat (about ⅛-inch pieces—a daunting task), but using coarsely ground lamb shoulder works well too, and saves time.

WINE PAIRING: TORRE MIGLIORI MONTEPULCIANO D'ABRUZZO

For the ragù:

¼ cup extra-virgin olive oil
4 garlic cloves, thinly sliced
1 bay leaf
1 tablespoon minced fresh rosemary
¼ teaspoon red pepper flakes
¾ pound coarsely ground or very finely minced lamb shoulder
1 teaspoon salt

½ teaspoon freshly ground black pepper
1 cup dry white wine
½ small yellow onion, thinly sliced
4 yellow bell peppers, seeded and cut into long, thin strips (about 2 pounds)
1 cup chopped San Marzano canned tomatoes
1 cup water, plus extra as needed

For the pasta:

2 tablespoons salt
1 pound maccheroni alla chitarra, bucatini, or spaghetti

1 cup (¼ pound) freshly grated Pecorino Romano

Make the ragù: In a heavy-bottomed saucepan large enough to accommodate the pasta, add 2 tablespoons of the olive oil, the garlic, bay leaf, rosemary, and red pepper flakes and set over medium-high heat. Cook for 1 minute. Add the lamb and cook for about 10 minutes, stirring often to break it up into tiny pieces, until thoroughly browned all over. Season with the salt and black pepper. It is crucial at this step to really brown the meat; if this step is rushed, the ragù will taste bland. Deglaze with the wine; when the wine almost fully evaporated, after about 3 minutes, add the onion and bell peppers. Cook for about 5 minutes, or until the vegetables soften. Add the tomatoes and water, cover, and reduce the heat to low; simmer and cook for about 2 hours, or until a rich sauce forms and the lamb is very tender, stirring occasionally and adding a little water as needed to maintain about ½ cup of liquid in the pan at all times. Adjust the seasoning if needed; discard the bay leaf and keep warm. (The sauce can be made up to this point 2 days in advance; refrigerate until needed, then warm gently before proceeding.)

Make the pasta: Bring 5 quarts of water to a boil. Add the salt and the pasta. Cook until the pasta is al dente, then drain, reserving 2 cups of the pasta cooking water.

To serve: Toss the pasta with the ragù and the remaining 2 tablespoons of olive oil. Sauté over high heat for 1 minute to meld the flavors, thinning out the sauce as needed with some of the reserved pasta cooking water. Adjust the seasoning, sprinkle with the Pecorino, and serve hot.

The Easy Way to Roast Peppers

Roasting peppers can be a daunting task, but not if you do it this way: cut the peppers in half, seed them, and place them on an aluminum foil–lined rimmed baking sheet; broil them in a preheated oven for about 15 minutes, until black and blistered. Remove from the oven, wrap to enclose in the foil, then peel away the skin once they're cool enough to handle. This is so much easier than roasting the peppers whole, and cleanup is a breeze.

Simple Lentil Sauce

Sugo di Lenticchie Pasta and lentils are a classic duet in central and southern Italy. Some recipes feature carrots, onions, celery, and tomatoes; while they too are delicious, they mask the earthy character of lentils. This streamlined recipe from Abruzzo calls for little other than lentils, pancetta, onions, rosemary, garlic, and bay leaves. SERVES 4

Ingredient notes: French lentils (du Puy) are good, but if you can, seek out Italian lentils, such as those from Castelluccio in Umbria. Unlike dried beans or chickpeas, dried lentils do not require overnight soaking; just rinse, pick them over, and cook for about 1 hour. Orange lentils won't work, as they cook through in 10 minutes and become very soft.

WINE PAIRING: LA VALENTINA PECORINO

For the sauce:

1 cup dried brown or green lentils, rinsed and picked over

2 medium yellow onions, 1 thinly sliced and 1 minced

2 bay leaves

1 teaspoon salt

¼ cup extra-virgin olive oil

3 ounces pancetta, finely diced

2 garlic cloves, minced

1 tablespoon minced fresh rosemary

½ teaspoon freshly ground black pepper

For the pasta:

2 tablespoons salt

1 pound gemelli or strozzapreti

Make the sauce: In a large pot, place the lentils and add enough cool water to cover. Add the sliced onion and the bay leaves. Season with 1 teaspoon of the salt. Set over medium heat and cook for about 1 hour, until the lentils are tender. Drain the lentils and reserve the lentil cooking liquid. Set aside.

In a heavy saucepan large enough to accommodate the pasta, sauté 2 tablespoons of the olive oil and the minced onion, pancetta, garlic, and rosemary over medium heat for about 5 minutes, until aromatic, being careful not to brown the onion or pancetta; a little golden color is fine. Stir in the drained cooked lentils and the bay leaves. Pour in 1 cup of the reserved lentil cooking liquid, season with the pepper, reduce the heat to low, and cover; cook for 1 hour, stirring often and adding a bit of the lentil cooking liquid as needed to keep the sauce moist. The lentils will have broken down a bit and the sauce will be thick and viscous; that is fine. Adjust the seasoning and keep warm. (The sauce can be made up to this point 2 days in advance; refrigerate until needed, then warm gently before proceeding.)

Make the pasta: Bring 5 quarts of water to a boil. Add the salt and the pasta. Cook until the pasta is almost but not quite al dente, then drain, reserving 2 cups of the pasta cooking water.

To serve: Add the pasta to the sauce and sauté over high heat for about 2 minutes, or until the pasta is al dente, adding some of the reserved lentil cooking liquid (or, if that is finished, the reserved pasta cooking water) as needed to thin out the sauce. Stir in the remaining 2 tablespoons of olive oil. Discard the bay leaves. Adjust the seasoning and serve hot.

Pastas to Enjoy at Room Temperature

Most pastas are best eaten hot—as soon as they are ready, in fact. But some are even better savored at room temperature, and these lend themselves to summertime entertaining or lazy nights at home. Here are the recipes in this book that taste just as good, or better, at room temperature:

- Slow-Cooked Cranberry Bean Sauce with Scallions, Pancetta, and Garlic-Parsley Garnish (page 37)
- Tuna, Anchovy, and Olive Sauce with Fresh Tomatoes (page 96)
- Fragrant Garlic and Parsley Sauce (page 103)
- Simple Lentil Sauce (page 135)
- Garlic-Laced Broccoli Sauce (page 147)
- Wild Chickpea Purée with Garlic-Chili Oil (page 149)
- Crushed Asparagus Sauce (page 151)
- Summer Tomato Sauce with Basil and Lemon (page 167)
- Chunky Chickpea Sauce (page 162)
- Quick and Fiery Tomato Sauce with Olives, Capers, and Anchovies (page 172)
- Roasted Pepper Sauce with Eggplant, Tomatoes, and Olives (page 207)

Tomato Sauce with Tiny Meatballs Teramo-Style

Sugo di Pomodoro con Polpettine alla Teramana Pasta and meatballs is hardly a commonplace dish in Italy—it is mostly in southern Italy that meatballs are simmered in tomato sauce, to be tossed with pasta. But the meatballs are usually small (about the size of a walnut), and there are never more than a few meatballs per serving of pasta. It is once they reached America that Italian immigrants—who came to America in the early 1900s, used to a life of poverty and a dearth of ingredients back home—made their meatballs larger, their sauce richer. Here is the way pasta with meatballs appears in Abruzzo. SERVES 4

Ingredient notes: Use any combination of ground meat you like; I prefer half pork shoulder and half beef chuck.

WINE PAIRING: CANTINE TALAMONTI KUDOS

For the meatballs:

½ cup packed torn, day-old crustless bread (measure after removing the crusts and tearing)

¼ cup whole or 2% milk

1 large egg

1¼ teaspoons salt

½ teaspoon freshly ground black pepper

2 garlic cloves, minced

2 tablespoons minced fresh flat-leaf parsley

¼ teaspoon freshly grated nutmeg

½ pound coarsely ground pork shoulder

½ pound coarsely ground beef chuck

For the sauce:

2 tablespoons extra-virgin olive oil

1 medium yellow onion, minced (about ½ cup)

2 garlic cloves, minced

1 tablespoon minced fresh flat-leaf parsley

¼ teaspoon red pepper flakes

2 cups chopped San Marzano canned tomatoes

1 cup water, plus extra as needed

1 teaspoon salt

½ teaspoon freshly ground black pepper

8 fresh basil leaves, torn

For the pasta:

2 tablespoons salt
I pound rigatoni, maccheroni alla chitarra,
   or mezzi rigatoni

Freshly grated Pecorino Romano for passing
   at the table

Make the meatballs: In a large bowl, soak the bread in the milk for 5 minutes. Add the egg, salt, pepper, garlic, parsley, and nutmeg. Mash with your hands until well mixed. (By mixing the seasonings into the bread mixture, rather than the meat, you ensure that all of the meat will be evenly seasoned.) Add the pork and beef chuck. Knead well for 2 minutes; the mixture will be sticky. With lightly moistened hands, roll into walnut-size balls and place on a rimmed baking sheet. Cover and refrigerate. (This can be done up to 24 hours before cooking.)

Make the sauce: In a wide saucepan large enough to accommodate the meatballs in a single layer (this is very important if the meatballs are to cook through evenly), as well as the pasta, combine the olive oil, onion, garlic, parsley, and red pepper flakes. Set over medium heat and cook, stirring occasionally, for about 5 minutes, until the onion becomes translucent. Add the tomatoes, water, salt, and black pepper and bring to a gentle boil. Cover and simmer for about 30 minutes, or until the sauce takes on a rich orange hue, adding water as needed to keep the consistency loose. Uncover, and gently drop in the meatballs one by one in a single layer. Use a spoon to gently turn the meatballs, coating them in sauce. Return the sauce to a gentle boil, cover, and cook for 30 minutes, occasionally shaking the pan to move the meatballs around and adding a bit of water as needed to keep the meatballs barely covered in sauce. (The sauce can be made up to this point 2 days in advance; refrigerate until needed, then warm gently before proceeding.) Stir in the basil, adjust the seasoning, and keep warm.

Make the pasta: Bring 5 quarts of water to a boil. Add the salt and the pasta. Cook until the pasta is al dente, then drain, reserving 2 cups of the pasta cooking water.

To serve: Add the drained pasta to the sauce and sauté over medium heat for I minute to meld the flavors, being careful not to break the meatballs, thinning out the sauce as needed with some of the reserved pasta cooking water. Adjust the seasoning and serve hot, passing the Pecorino at the table.

Fresh Ricotta Sauce with Diced Prosciutto

Salsa di Ricotta con Dadini di Prosciutto Three ingredients, and you have an amazing meal in minutes. You don't even need a pot or pan to cook the sauce for this country-style Abruzzese pasta. **SERVES 4**

Ingredient notes: Fresh ricotta cheese from a cheese shop is necessary for the correct consistency and creaminess; if all you have access to is supermarket ricotta cheese, drain it in a cheesecloth-lined sieve over a bowl for a few hours, then stir in a few tablespoons of heavy cream to round out the flavors.

WINE PAIRING: CATALDI MADONNA TREBBIANO D'ABRUZZO

For the pasta:

2 tablespoons salt

1 pound maccheroni alla chitarra, farfalle, or spaghetti

For the sauce:

10 ounces fresh whole-milk ricotta cheese

½ cup (2 ounces) freshly grated Pecorino Romano

¼ pound prosciutto di Parma in one thick slice, cut into ⅛-inch dice

¼ teaspoon freshly ground black pepper, or more to taste

Salt as needed

Make the pasta: Bring 5 quarts of water to a boil. Add the salt and the pasta. Cook until the pasta is al dente, then drain, reserving 2 cups of the pasta cooking water.

Meanwhile, make the sauce: In a bowl large enough to accommodate the pasta, place the ricotta. Stir in the Pecorino, prosciutto, and pepper. Taste for salt and add as needed. Set aside.

To serve: Stir 1 cup of the reserved pasta cooking water into the ricotta mixture in the bowl, thereby making it more fluid. Add the drained pasta and stir vigorously to coat. Add more of the reserved pasta cooking water as needed to thin out the sauce. Adjust the seasoning and serve hot.

Molise

If you like chilies, garlic, and olive oil, you'll love the cooking of this small southern region that borders Abruzzo to the north and Apulia to the south. Most of the classic pasta sauces here start with these three ingredients, and pancetta (or fatback, in the old days) usually provides extra flavor and richness. Molise's cuisine is a peasant one: historically a poor region, it belonged to Abruzzo until the 1960s, and indeed there are many similarities between Molise's and Abruzzo's dishes. Celery, beans, tomatoes, potatoes, and onions frequently turn up in everyday pasta sauces, and long-simmered ragùs take center stage when a feast is in order. Molise's coastline may be short, but it offers an abundance of fish and seafood: clams, mussels, baby squid the size of a thumbnail, cuttlefish, and all manner of saltwater fish are cooked simply with white wine and parsley as a hearty sauce for pasta. Some pasta sauces are slow-cooked in terra-cotta pots, where they acquire deep flavor and character.

Spicy Cannellini Bean Sauce with Pancetta and Arugula

Malefante In Molise, where celery is prized and pork is a staple, white beans are cooked with celery and pork rind until tender. I prefer the flavor of pancetta, which is less fatty than pork rind and more aromatic. SERVES 4

> **Ingredient notes:** Dried beans can be used in place of canned beans, but allow time for overnight soaking and longer boiling; use ¾ pound of dried cannellini beans, soak them in cool water to cover overnight, then drain and simmer with fresh water to cover for about 2 hours, until tender.

WINE PAIRING: DI MAJO NORANTE CONTADO AGLIANICO DEL MOLISE RISERVA

For the sauce:

2 tablespoons plus ¼ cup extra-virgin olive oil
1 large yellow onion, minced (about 1 cup)
2 celery stalks, minced (about 1 cup)
6 garlic cloves, minced
¼ pound pancetta, cut into ¼-inch dice
½ teaspoon red pepper flakes

3 15.5-ounce cans cannellini beans, drained and rinsed
2 cups water, plus extra as needed
1 bay leaf
1 teaspoon salt
¼ teaspoon freshly ground black pepper

For the pasta:

2 tablespoons salt
1 pound sedanini, cavatappi, or tubetti

¼ pound arugula leaves

Make the sauce: In a deep, wide saucepan large enough to accommodate the pasta, place 2 tablespoons of the olive oil and the onion, celery, garlic, pancetta, and red pepper flakes. Cook over medium heat for about 10 minutes, until the onion and celery become translucent and the pancetta renders its fat. Stir in the beans and pour in the water. Submerge the bay leaf in the liquid and season with the salt and black pepper. Bring to a gentle boil and cover. Cook over medium-low heat for about 1 hour, until the beans are very tender and the sauce has thickened, adding water as needed. Use a fork or large spoon to crush about half of the beans into a thick purée. Adjust the seasoning and keep warm. (The sauce can be made up to this point 2 days in advance; refrigerate until needed, then warm gently before proceeding.)

Make the pasta: Bring 5 quarts of water to a boil. Add the salt and the pasta. Cook until the pasta is almost but not quite al dente, then drain, reserving 2 cups of the pasta cooking water. The pasta will finish cooking in the sauce.

To serve: Stir the drained pasta into the sauce and sauté over high heat for about 2 minutes, stirring constantly and thinning out the sauce as needed with some of the reserved pasta cooking water, until the pasta is al dente and the sauce coats the pasta well. Stir in the remaining ¼ cup of olive oil and the arugula and toss well so that the arugula wilts and becomes an integral part of the sauce. Discard the bay leaf. Adjust the seasoning and serve hot.

Pancetta and Cousins

Italian bacon is generally unsmoked: called pancetta, it is named after the belly (pancia) of the pig and is available either rolled in a spiral or flat; it has a more delicate flavor than American smoked bacon. Guanciale, named after the cheeks (guancia) of the pig, is saltier, fattier, and more aromatic than pancetta and bacon. If you can't find pancetta or guanciale, use bacon instead, but the taste will be smokier.

Garlic-Laced Broccoli Sauce

Sugo di Broccoli Saltati all'Aglio e Peperoncino Southern Italians, and Molisani in particular, have a talent for marrying pasta and vegetables. For the deepest vegetal flavor, the broccoli shouldn't be crisp or bright green; rather, it should be limp after its sojourn in a hot pan with garlic, red pepper flakes, and olive oil. SERVES 4

> **Ingredient notes:** The sweetest broccoli has tightly woven florets without any hint of yellowing. The stems are edible, too, as long as they are peeled before slicing, and the bottom inch is discarded.

WINE PAIRING: DI MAJO NORANTE SANGIOVESE TERRE DEGLI OSCI

For the sauce:

2 tablespoons plus ½ teaspoon salt

2 large bunches of broccoli, stems trimmed, cut or torn into tiny florets (about 1½ pounds trimmed weight)

2 tablespoons plus ¼ cup extra-virgin olive oil

4 garlic cloves, minced

½ teaspoon red pepper flakes

For the pasta:

1 pound cavatelli or orecchiette

1 cup (¼ pound) freshly grated Pecorino Romano

Make the sauce: Bring 8 quarts of water to a boil. Add 2 tablespoons of the salt and the broccoli. Cook for about 2 minutes, or until the broccoli is just crisp-tender; using a slotted spoon, remove the broccoli to a bowl of ice water and set aside until cool, then drain. Reserve the pot of salted water.

In a saucepan large enough to accommodate the pasta, place 2 tablespoons of the olive oil, the garlic, and the red pepper flakes. Set over medium heat and cook very gently, without allowing the garlic to take on any color, for 30 seconds to 1 minute, until the oil is aromatic. Add the broccoli and sauté for about 10 minutes, stirring often, until the broccoli is permeated with the aroma of garlic and red pepper flakes and is a bit limp around the edges. Season with the remaining ½ teaspoon of salt and keep warm. (The sauce can be made up to this point 2 days in advance; refrigerate until needed, then warm gently before proceeding.)

Make the pasta: Return the broccoli cooking water to a boil. Add the pasta to the pot. Cook until the pasta is al dente, then drain, reserving 2 cups of the pasta cooking water.

To serve: Add the drained pasta to the saucepan with the broccoli. Stir in the remaining ¼ cup of olive oil and the Pecorino. Sauté over high heat for 1 minute to meld the flavors, thinning out the sauce as needed with some of the reserved pasta cooking water. Adjust the seasoning and serve hot.

Wild Chickpea Purée with Garlic-Chili Oil

Sugo di Cicerchie If you're looking for the quintessential pasta e fagioli—that rich, comforting combination of pasta with beans that generations of Italians have been sustained by—this Molisano version is it. You'll need to soak the cicerchie overnight in cool water to cover, so do plan ahead. SERVES 4

> **Ingredient notes:** Cicerchie are wild chickpeas, and they have a delicate, sweet flavor; seek them out at specialty Italian markets (see page 229) but it's worth every bit of effort at tracking them down. Soaking overnight and slipping off their papery skins will be amply rewarded by a dish unlike any pasta e fagioli you've ever tasted.

WINE PAIRING: DI MAJO NORANTE DON LUIGI MONTEPULCIANO DEL MOLISE RISERVA

For the sauce:

6 ounces dried cicerchie (or, if unavailable, dried chickpeas)

4 cups cool water, plus extra as needed

½ large yellow onion, peeled

1 bay leaf

1 ½ teaspoons salt

For the chili-garlic oil:

¼ cup extra-virgin olive oil

3 garlic cloves, thinly sliced

3 dried chili peppers, crumbled, or ½ teaspoon red pepper flakes

For the pasta:

2 tablespoons salt

1 pound orecchiette or mezzi rigatoni

Make the sauce: Rinse and pick over the cicerchie to get rid of small stones and grit. Place the cicerchie in a bowl and cover with cool water. Discard any cicerchie that rise to the top. Cover and allow to soak overnight.

Drain the cicerchie and slip off the thin outer skin from each; this is very important as the skins are inedible. In a 3-quart pot, place the shucked cicerchie. Add the water; if needed, add more water to cover the cicerchie by 1 inch. Add the onion and bay leaf. Season with the salt and bring to a boil over medium-high heat. Cover, reduce the heat to low, and cook for about 1 ½ hours, until the cicerchie are tender, adding water as needed to keep the sauce moist. Occasionally, using the back of a slotted spoon, crush the cicerchie so that they eventually form a thick purée. If you want the sauce more velvety, purée with an immersion blender or transfer in batches to a blender or food processor. Discard the bay leaf and adjust the seasoning as needed; the onion will have pretty much disintegrated into the sauce. Keep warm. (The sauce can be made up to this point 2 days in advance; refrigerate until needed, then warm gently before proceeding.)

Make the chili-garlic oil: In a small pan, place the olive oil, garlic, and chili and warm gently over low heat for about 2 minutes, until infused. The garlic should not take on any color or it will turn bitter. Set aside.

Make the pasta: Bring 5 quarts of water to a boil. Add the salt and the pasta. Cook the pasta until almost but not quite al dente, then drain, reserving 2 cups of the pasta cooking water.

To serve: Stir the pasta into the sauce. Add as much of the reserved pasta cooking water as needed to dilute the sauce to a thick soup-like consistency (depending on how thick or thin the sauce was, you may or may not need any pasta cooking water). Sauté over high heat, stirring constantly, for about 2 minutes, until the pasta is al dente and the sauce has thickened nicely and coats the pasta well. Adjust the seasoning, drizzle with the chili-garlic oil, and serve hot.

A Little Bit of Heat Goes a Long Way

Sometimes all a dish needs to really shine is a little extra seasoning. When you taste a finished dish and aren't quite getting excited at the flavors, salt is usually what's missing; but sometimes, just a touch of heat will pull all the disparate elements together and provide a needed shot of flavor. I find a touch of good-quality crushed red pepper flakes (ideally Calabrese) really adds a lot when sprinkled on or folded in just before serving. Red pepper flakes marry well with anything except creamy, delicate sauces, and the quantity you add depends on your heat tolerance.

Crushed Asparagus Sauce

Sugo di Asparagi Disfatti I first enjoyed this dish at the home of a wine-making family in Campomarino. Looking at the pasta as it was brought to the table, I was less than inspired: the asparagus sauce was a dull khaki green. And then I tasted it: the asparagus had cooked into a subtle, delicate mass, losing its bright edge, gaining a depth I never suspected it possessed. SERVES 4

Ingredient notes: Thick or thin, it doesn't matter: choose the best-looking asparagus for this dish. Check the tips: they should be closed tightly, like a flower, and show no trace of wetness. The stalk should be firm and snappy, and the bottom not desiccated.

WINE PAIRING: BORGO DI COLLOREDO GIRONIA BIFERNO BIANCO

For the sauce:

2 pounds asparagus (2 large bunches)
2 tablespoons plus ¼ cup extra-virgin olive oil
1 medium yellow onion, minced (about ½ cup)

1 teaspoon salt
¼ teaspoon freshly ground black pepper
2 cups water, plus extra as needed

For the pasta:

2 tablespoons salt

1 pound fresh egg tagliatelle or orecchiette

Make the sauce: Cut the bottom inch from each stalk of asparagus and discard. Cut off the tips right where they meet the stalks and, using a small paring knife, cut the tips in half lengthwise; reserve the tips to cook later along with the pasta, as a garnish.

Using a vegetable peeler, peel the fibrous outer layer from the pared asparagus stalks, starting at the bottom and going about 3 inches up; this will make the asparagus much more tender and will promote the puréeing of the asparagus while the sauce cooks. Cut the trimmed and pared asparagus stalks into ¼-inch lengths and set aside.

In a saucepan large enough to accommodate the pasta, place 2 tablespoons of the olive oil. Add the onion and cook over medium heat for about 5 minutes, or until the onion is translucent; the onion should not brown. Add the chopped asparagus stalks, the salt, pepper, and water. Cook, covered, for 45 minutes, crushing the asparagus against the pan with a fork or a large slotted spoon every few minutes and adding as much water as needed to keep the sauce moist. The asparagus should form a chunky purée. It will be a muted khaki color, not at all vibrant and vivacious. Adjust the seasoning and keep warm. (The sauce can be made up to this point 2 days in advance; refrigerate until needed, then warm gently before proceeding.)

Make the pasta: Bring 5 quarts of water to a boil. Add the reserved asparagus tips, the salt, and the pasta. Cook until the pasta is almost but not quite al dente, then drain, reserving 2 cups of the pasta cooking water.

To serve: Stir the pasta and the reserved asparagus tips into the sauce. Add as much of the reserved pasta cooking water as needed to dilute the sauce to a thick soup-like consistency. Sauté over high heat for about 2 minutes, stirring constantly, until the pasta is al dente. Stir in the remaining ¼ cup of olive oil. Adjust the seasoning and serve hot.

Ten Ingredients You Can't Do Without

Every dish is only as good as the ingredients that go into it. It really pays off to look for the best possible ingredients (and this does not always mean the most expensive ingredients). Here are the ten items you really can't do without in your Italian kitchen:

1. Imported Italian pasta (or freshly made if you are up for it, see pages 223–228; or if you can find a good source in your area)
2. Fruity extra-virgin olive oil
3. A chunk of Parmigiano-Reggiano or Grana Padano
4. A wedge of Pecorino Romano
5. Authentic San Marzano canned tomatoes
6. Unsalted butter (preferably imported from France or Italy)
7. A firm head of garlic
8. Fine sea salt
9. Fragrant dried red pepper flakes
10. Freshly ground black pepper (preferably Tellicherry)

Apulia

One of Italy's least hilly regions, Apulia is blessed with a mild climate that ensures an abundance of fresh produce and thriving olive trees. Not surprisingly, most daily meals in Apulia center around pasta with vegetables and olive oil. The durum wheat grown in the sprawling Tavoliere Plain is milled into semolina flour for every shape of pasta imaginable: long, short, rounded, ridged, concave. Cavatelli and orecchiette are Apulia's most typical pasta shapes, made skillfully by hand in both country and city homes. Since most Apulian pasta is made only of semolina flour and water without any eggs, it pairs best with hearty, garlic-scented vegetable sauces featuring cauliflower, celery, potatoes, broccoli raab, arugula, tomatoes, peppers, or wild greens gathered in the countryside. There are also rich, slow-simmered meat sauces, and along the glittering coastline, the local seafood is transformed into simple, satisfying pasta sauces.

White Clam Sauce

Sugo di Vongole in Bianco There are two ways to serve pasta with mussels or clams in Italy: red (with tomatoes) or white (without). I find that adding tomatoes makes the taste of the seafood less distinctive. Here is a classic Apulian way of saucing pasta: clams or cockles cooked in olive oil with white wine, garlic, and parsley, seasoned simply with salt and freshly ground black pepper. The same can be done with mussels. SERVES 4

Ingredient notes: Italian clams (vongole) are small and delicate, their flavor briny and sweet. They are more similar to cockles (a New Zealand bivalve with a pretty greenish-gray shell) than to American clams. Any cockles that are yawning open prior to cooking should be tapped to see if they close; if they do not close, discard them before cooking. If using American clams, reduce the amount of salt to 1 tablespoon for soaking and ⅛ teaspoon for sautéing.

WINE PAIRING: REALE ALISEO BIANCO COLLI DI SALERNO

For the sauce:

4 pounds New Zealand cockles, scrubbed
2 tablespoons plus ½ teaspoon salt
½ cup dry white wine

6 tablespoons extra-virgin olive oil
2 garlic cloves, minced
½ teaspoon freshly ground black pepper

For the pasta:

2 tablespoons salt
1 pound spaghetti

2 tablespoons minced fresh flat-leaf parsley

Make the sauce: Rinse the cockles several times to get rid of any surface grit. In a deep bowl, place the cockles and cover with cool water. Add 2 tablespoons of the salt and swirl with your hands to dissolve the salt in the water. Set aside for 30 minutes at room temperature, to purge any remaining sediment and grit. Remove the cockles from their soaking water by scooping them out with your hands, thereby avoiding disturbing the sediment at the bottom of the bowl. Rinse the cockles several times in cool water.

    In a saucepan large enough to accommodate the pasta, place the cockles and the wine and cover with a tight-fitting lid. Cook over medium-high heat for about 10 minutes, shaking the pan occasionally, until the cockles open. Cool for 5 minutes, then remove the cockles from their shells. Discard the shells. Also be sure to discard any unopened cockles. Reserve the cooking juices; pour the juices through a sieve lined with paper towels (or through a coffee filter) into a bowl, being careful not to pour out all the juices, as the sediment will inevitably settle at the bottom of the pan. Reserve the filtered juices. Rinse out the saucepan and dry it.

In the same saucepan, place 3 tablespoons of the olive oil and the garlic over medium-high heat. Cook for about 30 seconds, until aromatic. Add the shelled cockles and their filtered juices and cook for about 2 minutes. Season with the remaining ½ teaspoon of salt and the pepper. Adjust the seasoning and keep warm.

Make the pasta: Bring 5 quarts of water to a boil. Add the salt and the pasta. Cook until the pasta is al dente, then drain, reserving 2 cups of the pasta cooking water.

To serve: Toss the drained pasta, parsley, and the remaining 3 tablespoons of olive oil into the sauce. Sauté over high heat for 1 minute to meld the flavors, thinning out the sauce as needed with some of the reserved pasta cooking water. Adjust the seasoning and serve hot.

Oven-Roasted Tomato and Bread Crumb Sauce

Sugo di Pomodorini Gratinati This Apulian sauce is so good that I suggest you make twice what you need and serve the rest as a topping for grilled fish, polenta, or crostini. Alternately, if you cook the sauce for half as long as indicated below, the tomatoes will remain intact, making a lovely side dish for meat or poultry, so you can easily double the sauce and pull half of it out of the oven for use the next day as a side dish. SERVES 4

> **Ingredient notes:** Only the ripest, juiciest summer tomatoes will do justice to this sauce. If the beefsteak tomatoes look more promising than the plum tomatoes, by all means, use those instead.

WINE PAIRING: PAOLO PETRILLI AGRAMANTE CACC'E MMITTE DI LUCERA

For the bread crumbs:

I tablespoon extra-virgin olive oil

I garlic clove, minced

½ cup coarse homemade bread crumbs or unflavored bread crumbs, such as panko

¼ teaspoon salt

¼ teaspoon freshly ground black pepper

For the sauce:

2 tablespoons plus ¼ cup extra-virgin olive oil, plus extra for greasing the roasting pan

2 pounds ripe tomatoes, cored, halved, and seeded

I teaspoon salt

¼ teaspoon freshly ground black pepper, plus extra for serving

2 garlic cloves, minced

For the pasta:

2 tablespoons salt

I pound zite, bucatini, or mezzi rigatoni

2 tablespoons minced fresh oregano or I teaspoon dried oregano

Make the bread crumbs: Place the olive oil and garlic in a small skillet and warm over medium heat for about I minute, until aromatic. Add the bread crumbs, salt, and pepper and cook, stirring often, for about 5 minutes, until the bread crumbs are a very light golden color. Transfer to a bowl.

Make the sauce: Preheat the oven to 375°F.

Lightly oil a large, heavy roasting pan with olive oil. Arrange the tomatoes in the pan, cut side up, and season with the salt and pepper. Sprinkle with 2 tablespoons of the olive oil, the garlic, and the bread crumbs. Roast in the preheated oven for about 40 minutes, or until the tomatoes start to burst a bit and the bread crumbs are golden brown. Remove from the oven and cover the tomatoes with aluminum foil if needed to keep warm while you cook the pasta. (The sauce can be made up to this point 2 days in advance; refrigerate until needed, then warm gently in a low oven to crisp up the bread crumbs and warm the tomatoes before proceeding.)

Make the pasta: Bring 5 quarts of water to a boil. Add the salt and the pasta. Cook until the pasta is al dente, then drain, reserving 2 cups of the pasta cooking water.

To serve: Transfer the drained pasta, the remaining ¼ cup of olive oil, the oregano, and pepper to the hot roasting pan with the tomatoes. Toss vigorously with tongs to coat the pasta thoroughly with the juices in the pan and to crush the tomatoes, thinning out the sauce as needed with some of the reserved pasta cooking water. Adjust the seasoning and serve hot.

Sunday Braciole Sauce

Sugo di Braciole di Manzo This is Sunday food in Apulia: beef is pounded thin and rolled around pancetta, parsley, garlic, and grated Pecorino, then braised with red wine and tomatoes until succulent. In Italian fashion, the stuffed beef (known as *braciole* in southern Italy, *involtini* in northern Italy) is served as a second course, its rich cooking juices tossed with pasta as a first course. SERVES 4

Ingredient notes: Most recipes for braciole call for flank steak; I have found the resulting bundles tough, as flank is very lean, and best grilled or quickly stir-fried. For melt-in-the-mouth tender braciole, ask your butcher for beef round tip steak; it is a cut next to the sirloin.

WINE PAIRING: LEONE DE CASTRIS DONNA LISA SALICE SALENTINO ROSSO RISERVA

For the bundles:

1½ pounds beef round tip steak, cut into 2 pieces and pounded thin with a mallet (about ¼ inch thick)

½ teaspoon salt

½ teaspoon freshly ground black pepper

¼ pound pancetta, finely minced

4 garlic cloves, finely minced

¼ cup coarsely chopped fresh flat-leaf parsley

½ cup (2 ounces) freshly grated Pecorino Romano

For the sauce:

2 tablespoons extra-virgin olive oil

1 large yellow onion, thinly sliced

¼ teaspoon red pepper flakes

1 cup dry red wine

1 teaspoon salt

¼ teaspoon freshly ground black pepper

2 cups chopped San Marzano canned tomatoes

1 cup water, plus extra as needed

For the pasta:

2 tablespoons salt

1 pound orecchiette or cavatelli

1 cup (¼ pound) freshly grated Pecorino Romano

Make the bundles: Line a counter with a sheet of aluminum foil or parchment paper and place the two slices of steak on the foil or parchment in a single layer. Season evenly with the salt and pepper. In a bowl, combine the pancetta, garlic, parsley, and Pecorino. Spread the pancetta mixture evenly over the meat. Following the natural grain of the meat, roll the meat into tight bundles and tie with kitchen string. The meat will be more tender once cooked if you roll with the grain instead of against the grain, so that when you slice the braciole later, it will be against the grain.

Make the sauce: In a deep, wide saucepan large enough to accommodate the pasta, warm the olive oil over medium heat. Add the bundles and cook, turning as needed, for about 10 minutes, until the bundles brown evenly on all sides. (Don't worry if a bit of the stuffing pops out while searing; it will add richness to the sauce.) Stir in the onion and red pepper flakes and cook for about 5 minutes, until the onion is translucent and lightly golden. Deglaze with the wine and cook for about 3 minutes, until the wine almost fully evaporates, scraping the bottom of the pan to release any bits and pieces that have stuck. Add the salt and pepper and stir in the tomatoes and water. Bring to a gentle boil. Cover and cook over low heat for 1 to 2 hours, or until the bundles feel tender when poked with a fork. Add a bit of water as needed to prevent scorching and to keep the sauce moist, turning the bundles occasionally to promote even cooking. Taste the sauce and adjust the seasoning. Remove the bundles from the sauce, discard the string, and place on a platter with a bit of the sauce; cover with foil and set aside to enjoy as a second course. Keep the sauce warm. (The sauce can be made up to this point 2 days in advance; refrigerate until needed, then warm gently before proceeding.)

Make the pasta: Bring 5 quarts of water to a boil. Add the salt and the pasta. Cook until the pasta is al dente, then drain and place the pasta in a large bowl, reserving 2 cups of the pasta cooking water.

To serve: Toss the pasta into the sauce and stir in the Pecorino. Sauté over high heat for 1 minute to meld the flavors, thinning out the sauce as needed with some of the reserved pasta cooking water. Adjust the seasoning and serve hot. Serve the bundles as a second course, thinly sliced and drizzled with some of the sauce.

Chunky Chickpea Sauce

S ugo di Ceci con Aglio ed Alloro Chickpeas, beans, and lentils have long been staple foods in Italy, and sauces such as this ensured that laborers and workers in Apulia made it through the day without hunger. SERVES 4

> **Ingredient notes:** You can soak and boil dried chickpeas if you prefer them to canned: pick 9 ounces of dried chickpeas over, soak them overnight in cool water to cover, drain, and boil them in fresh water for about 2 hours, until tender.

WINE PAIRING: SANTA LUCIA VIGNA DEL MELOGRANO CASTEL DEL MONTE

For the sauce:

2 15.5-ounce cans chickpeas, drained and rinsed repeatedly
2 cups water, plus extra as needed
2 tablespoons plus ¼ cup extra-virgin olive oil
4 garlic cloves, minced
¼ teaspoon red pepper flakes
1 large yellow onion, minced

2 tablespoons minced fresh oregano
12 fresh basil leaves, torn
2 bay leaves
½ pound ripe tomatoes, cut into ½-inch dice
1 teaspoon salt
¼ teaspoon freshly ground black pepper, plus extra for serving

For the pasta:

2 tablespoons salt

1 pound tubetti or sedanini

Make the sauce: In the bowl of a food processor, process half of the chickpeas with 2 cups of water until smooth. Set aside.

In a saucepan large enough to accommodate the pasta, place 2 tablespoons of the olive oil, the garlic, and the red pepper flakes. Set over medium heat and warm gently for about 1 minute, or until aromatic. Add the onion, oregano, basil, and bay leaves and cook for about 5 minutes, or until the onion becomes translucent. Add the puréed and whole chickpeas, the tomatoes, salt, and black pepper. Cover, reduce the heat to medium-low, and cook for about 1 hour 15 minutes, or until the chickpeas are tender and the sauce has thickened; be sure to add more water as needed during cooking to keep enough moisture in the

(continued on page 164)

pan. The sauce should be somewhat soupy. Adjust the seasoning and keep warm. (The sauce can be made up to this point 2 days in advance; refrigerate until needed, then warm gently before proceeding.)

Make the pasta: Bring 5 quarts of water to a boil. Add the salt and the pasta. Cook until the pasta is almost but not quite al dente, then drain, reserving 2 cups of the pasta cooking water.

To serve: Stir the pasta into the chickpeas. Add as much of the reserved pasta cooking water as needed to dilute the sauce to a thick soup-like consistency. Sauté over high heat, stirring constantly, for about 2 minutes, until the pasta is al dente. Discard the bay leaves. Adjust the seasoning, drizzle with the remaining ¼ cup of olive oil, sprinkle with pepper, and serve hot.

Campania

Campania is best known around the world for its pizza, but cooks in the capital city of Naples and its surrounding towns and villages are masters at cooking pasta and at creating incredibly flavorful pasta sauces from relatively few and inexpensive ingredients. In fact, the Neapolitans were nicknamed *mangia-maccheroni* in the eighteenth century, when they ate pasta sold by street vendors with their right hands, tipping their heads back to better catch the noodles.

Most pasta sauces today are tomato-based, given the supreme quality of the local San Marzano tomatoes; capers, olives, and anchovies are frequently added for savor and bite. Spaghetti, bucatini, and vermicelli are the most common pasta shapes in Campania, ideally suited to quick-cooking, bright-tasting sauces. There are, of course, slow-simmered ragùs and hearty meat sauces for special days, but these are the exception rather than the rule.

Summer Tomato Sauce with Basil and Lemon

Salsa Estiva Fredda al Pomodoro con Limone e Basilico I am not usually a fan of pairing lemon with tomato, but in this summer sauce from Campania, the combination works beautifully. Taste for tartness before adding all of the lemon juice; you can always add more, but if you add too much, you'll have to incorporate more olive oil to balance the lemon's astringency, making the dish heavy rather than refreshing. SERVES 4

Ingredient notes: Whether you pick plum tomatoes, beefsteak tomatoes, or heirloom tomatoes, the cardinal rule is ripeness and juiciness.

WINE PAIRING: ALOIS AGLIANICO CAMPOLE

For the pasta:

2 tablespoons salt

1 pound spaghetti or spaghettini

For the sauce:

1¾ pounds ripe tomatoes, cored
2 garlic cloves
30 fresh basil leaves
1 teaspoon salt

⅓ cup extra-virgin olive oil
¼ teaspoon freshly ground black pepper
Juice of ½ lemon (about 2 tablespoons)

Make the pasta: Bring 5 quarts of water to a boil. Add the salt and the pasta. Cook until the pasta is al dente, then drain, reserving 2 cups of the pasta cooking water.

Meanwhile, make the sauce: Bring 1 quart of water to a boil. Have a large bowl of cool water handy by the pot of boiling water. Using a paring knife, cut an X into the bottom of each tomato. Drop the tomatoes into the boiling water; cook for about 30 seconds for ripe tomatoes and about 2 minutes for firmer tomatoes, until the skins begin to loosen. Drain the tomatoes. Place them in the bowl of cool water for 5 minutes, then drain them and slip off the skins. Cut the tomatoes in half crosswise and scoop out the seeds. Finely dice the tomatoes and set aside; collect any of the juices from the cutting board and add them to the diced tomatoes.

Place the garlic, basil, and salt on a cutting board and finely mince together; the salt will help keep the basil green after chopping. Stir the basil and garlic mixture into the tomatoes in the bowl. Add the olive oil and pepper and mix thoroughly. Stir in enough of the lemon juice to provide a pleasant tartness, but not so much that you overwhelm the flavor of the tomatoes and basil. The flavor of the lemon should not be distinctly discernible. Adjust the seasoning as needed.

To serve: Stir the drained pasta into the sauce in the bowl, thinning out the sauce as needed with some of the reserved pasta cooking water (it is likely, however, that the tomatoes are juicy enough that the sauce will not require any pasta cooking water). Adjust the seasoning. Serve hot, warm, or at room temperature. I prefer this pasta after it has had a chance to cool a bit: at room temperature, the sauce will have thickened slightly and the flavors melded.

Aglio, Olio, e Peperoncino: Southern Italy's Simplest Pasta Sauce

This is one of the simplest of pasta sauces: *aglio, olio, e peperoncino* translates as "garlic, oil, and chili pepper," and that is exactly what goes into it—no more and no less. Even grated cheese is frowned upon in most homes, as it masks the flavor of the spicy oil. To make pasta all'aglio, olio, e peperoncino, place ⅔ cup of extra-virgin olive oil, 4 sliced garlic cloves, and 2 crumbled dried chili peppers or 1 teaspoon (or more to taste) chili flakes in a small, heavy-bottomed skillet and warm gently over low heat until fragrant, about 5 minutes. Do not rush this step; the garlic should not brown and the oil should not shimmer or ripple, or the oil will taste bitter instead of sweet. Boil 1 pound of long pasta (typically spaghetti) and toss with the spiced oil and some pasta cooking water in a deep serving bowl, add salt if needed, and serve hot.

Classic Seafood Sauce

Sugo ai Frutti di Mare Here is a hearty, chunky Neapolitan sauce lightly flavored with tomatoes that marries splendidly with long pasta. SERVES 4

Ingredient notes: Mussels (such as clams, cockles, and all other bivalves) should be closed when purchased. If they are open before cooking, tap them on the inside of a bowl to see if they close; if they do not close, discard them. Similarly, mussels and other bivalves should open fully once cooked; any unopened ones should be discarded. If using American clams instead of cockles, reduce the amount of salt to 1 tablespoon for soaking and ⅛ teaspoon for sautéing.

WINE PAIRING: CLELIA ROMANO GRECO DI TUFO ALEXANDROS

For the sauce:

1 pound mussels, scrubbed, beards removed
1 pound cockles or littleneck clams, scrubbed
2 tablespoons plus ½ teaspoon salt
1 cup dry white wine
2 tablespoons plus ¼ cup extra-virgin olive oil
3 garlic cloves, minced
¼ cup minced fresh flat-leaf parsley

2 cups Fresh Tomato Sauce (page 221) or chopped San Marzano canned tomatoes
½ teaspoon freshly ground black pepper
½ pound cleaned squid, bodies sliced into rings
½ pound medium shrimp (41/50 are ideal for this), shelled and deveined

For the pasta:

2 tablespoons salt

1 pound spaghetti or spaghettini

Make the sauce: Rinse the mussels and cockles several times to get rid of any surface grit. In a deep bowl, place the mussels and cockles and cover with cool water. Add 2 tablespoons of the salt and swirl with your hands to dissolve the salt in the water. Set aside for 30 minutes at room temperature, to purge any sediment and grit. Remove the mussels and cockles from their soaking water by scooping them out with your hands, thereby avoiding disturbing the sediment at the bottom of the bowl. Rinse the mussels and cockles several times in cool water. Set aside.

In a pan large enough to accommodate the pasta, place the mussels and cockles. Pour in the wine and cover with a tight-fitting lid. Set over medium-high heat and cook for about

10 minutes, shaking the pan often, until the mussels and cockles open. Transfer the mussels and cockles to a bowl, discarding any that are unopened. Reserve the cooking juices; pour the juices through a sieve lined with paper towels (or through a coffee filter) into a bowl, being careful not to pour out all the juices, as the sediment will inevitably settle at the bottom of the pan. Reserve the filtered juices. Rinse and dry the saucepan.

In the same saucepan, place 2 tablespoons of the olive oil, two-thirds of the minced garlic, and half of the minced parsley and set it over medium-high heat. Cook for about 1 minute, until aromatic. Add the tomatoes, season with the remaining ½ teaspoon of salt and the pepper, and bring to a boil. Reduce the heat to medium-low and cook for 10 minutes. Stir in the mussels and cockles. Add 1 cup of the strained cooking liquid from the mussels and cockles, then stir in the squid. Cook, stirring often, for about 2 minutes, or until the squid is almost but not quite white all the way through. Stir in the shrimp and cook, stirring often, for about 2 minutes, or until the shrimp are fully cooked; do not overcook the shrimp, as they will become tough. Taste for seasoning and adjust as needed. Keep warm over a very low heat so as to avoid toughening the shrimp and squid.

Make the pasta: Bring 5 quarts of water to a boil. Add the salt and the pasta. Cook until the pasta is al dente, then drain, reserving 2 cups of the pasta cooking water.

To serve: Toss the drained pasta with the remaining parsley, the remaining garlic, and the remaining ¼ cup of olive oil into the sauce. Sauté over high heat for 1 minute to meld the flavors, thinning out the sauce as needed with some of the reserved pasta cooking water. Adjust the seasoning and serve hot.

Quick and Fiery Tomato Sauce with Olives, Capers, and Anchovies

Puttanesca This Neapolitan sauce is spicy, salty, garlicky—and absolutely addictive. It is quickly prepared and marries with short or long pasta, although spaghetti is its most common partner. SERVES 4

Ingredient notes: Many recipes for puttanesca include tomato paste, or concentrate, which makes for a sauce with a heavier, jammy taste. I prefer the lighter flavor without tomato paste.

WINE PAIRING: FEUDI DI SAN GREGORIO LACRYMA CHRISTI ROSSO

For the pasta:
2 tablespoons salt

1 pound spaghetti, fusilli lunghi, or penne

For the sauce:
¼ cup extra-virgin olive oil

1 dried red chili pepper, crumbled, or ¼ teaspoon red pepper flakes

2 garlic cloves, minced

8 oil-packed anchovy fillets, drained, or 4 salted anchovies, boned, gutted, and rinsed

2 cups Fresh Tomato Sauce (page 221) or chopped San Marzano canned tomatoes

½ cup water, plus extra as needed

2 tablespoons salted capers, rinsed and drained, or capers in brine, drained (chopped if large)

½ cup pitted gaeta or other oil-cured black olives, chopped

¼ teaspoon salt

Make the pasta: Bring 5 quarts of water to a boil. Add the salt and the pasta. Cook until the pasta is al dente, then drain, reserving 2 cups of the pasta cooking water.

Meanwhile, make the sauce: In a deep saucepan large enough to accommodate the pasta, place 2 tablespoons of the olive oil and the chili, garlic, and anchovies. Cook over medium-low heat for about 2 minutes, until the anchovies break down into a purée, crushing the anchovies with a fork or wooden spoon all the while. Don't rush this process or use too high a heat, as the anchovies may seize before they break down. Raise the temperature

(continued on page 174)

to medium-high and add the tomatoes, water, capers, olives, and salt; bring to a gentle boil and cover. Reduce the temperature to medium-low and cook for about 15 minutes, or until the tomatoes break down into a chunky sauce. Adjust the seasoning and keep warm. (The sauce can be made up to this point 2 days in advance; refrigerate until needed, then warm gently before proceeding.)

To serve: Toss the drained pasta with the sauce in the saucepan and sauté over high heat for 1 minute to meld the flavors, thinning out the sauce as needed with some of the reserved pasta cooking water. Adjust the seasoning, drizzle with the remaining 2 tablespoons of olive oil, and serve hot.

"Poor Man's" Garlic Bread Crumb Sauce

Sugo del Poverello When money was scarce and cheese too costly for the everyday table, Neapolitan cooks (and cooks in other southern Italian regions) toasted bread crumbs in olive oil as a substitute for grated cheese: it gave the pasta a textural contrast and savory note without much expense. SERVES 4

Ingredient notes: If homemade bread crumbs are unavailable, use panko bread crumbs instead; they have an airy, light texture that works well. Don't use flavored bread crumbs or finely ground packaged bread crumbs.

WINE PAIRING: PERILLO CODA DI VOLPE

For the pasta:

2 tablespoons salt

1 pound spaghetti

For the toasted bread crumbs:

4 slices day-old bread, or 2 cups unflavored bread crumbs, such as panko
1 garlic clove, halved lengthwise

2 tablespoons extra-virgin olive oil
¼ teaspoon salt

For the garlic oil:

⅓ cup extra-virgin olive oil
4 garlic cloves, minced

20 fresh basil leaves, torn

½ teaspoon freshly ground black pepper

1 teaspoon minced fresh oregano or
¼ teaspoon dried

Make the pasta: Bring 5 quarts of water to a boil. Add the salt and the pasta. Cook until the pasta is al dente, then drain, reserving 2 cups of the pasta cooking water.

Meanwhile, make the toasted bread crumbs: Rub the bread slices with the halved garlic clove on both sides until aromatic; tear the bread into tiny crumbs or pulse in the bowl of a food processor until it breaks down into crumbs; reserve the halved garlic clove. If you are not making homemade bread crumbs, use 2 cups panko bread crumbs instead. In a wide skillet, place the olive oil and reserved halved garlic clove and cook over medium heat for about 1 minute, until the garlic becomes golden; discard the garlic. Add the bread crumbs and season with the salt. Cook, stirring often, for about 5 minutes, until the bread crumbs are toasted all over and take on a light, nutty color. Transfer to a bowl and set aside.

Make the garlic oil: In the same skillet, place the olive oil and garlic and warm gently over low heat for about 5 minutes, until fragrant. Do not rush this step; the garlic should not brown and the oil should not shimmer or ripple, as the oil will taste bitter instead of sweet. Keep warm.

To serve: Transfer the drained pasta to a deep bowl and add the garlic oil. Toss vigorously with tongs to coat the pasta thoroughly with the garlic oil. Stir in the black pepper, basil, and oregano, thinning out the sauce as needed with some of the reserved pasta cooking water. Adjust the seasoning and serve hot, topped with the toasted bread crumbs.

The Old-Fashioned Way to Make Bread Crumbs

Once in a while, my husband decides to make bread crumbs the way his father, Attilio, always did: by taking a piece of stale bread and grating it on a box grater. This is the way most families made bread crumbs at home until a few decades ago. Nowadays, we can use a food processor to efficiently pulse the bread, resulting in a coarse or fine texture depending on how long we process the bread. Try the box grater method and you'll surely have a whole new respect for the work that went into cooking before electric gadgets eased our daily tasks!

Basilicata

One of Italy's poorest regions until a few decades ago, Basilicata is also one of Italy's least populated and most pristine: high, intractable mountains and arid soil made agriculture a difficult proposition in the area, and many *lucani* (as the people of Basilicata are called) immigrated to America and other countries in the early twentieth century in search of an easier life. While the economic situation is much improved today (largely thanks to petroleum extraction and tourism), the cuisine of Basilicata remains a peasant one, tied to its rural roots. The cooks in Basilicata are ingenious at turning a few simple ingredients into a memorable meal, often beginning the preparation of their classic pasta sauces with little more than dried chili peppers, garlic, and pork fat or olive oil. Some sauces call for pork sausage; others for lamb; others still for hearty vegetables such as broccoli raab or arugula. The result is always intensely savory and deeply satisfying.

Silky Broccoli Raab, Garlic, and Crushed Red Pepper Sauce

Sugo di Cime di Rape This recipe from Basilicata highlights how Italians cook down a key ingredient to create a sauce for pasta, without adding any liquid except pasta cooking water and olive oil. The trick is to cook the raab until it falls apart and becomes a silky, sweet purée. SERVES 4

Ingredient notes: Look for raab with no yellow buds, which are a sign of bitterness.

WINE PAIRING: BISCEGLIA TERRA DI VULCANO DRY MUSCAT

For the broccoli raab and pasta:

2 tablespoons salt

2 bunches of broccoli raab, tough stems removed, washed thoroughly, and chopped
1 pound cavatelli or orecchiette

For the garlic oil:

¼ cup extra-virgin olive oil
4 garlic cloves, minced
½ teaspoon red pepper flakes

1 cup (¼ pound) freshly grated Pecorino Romano
Salt as needed

Make the broccoli raab and pasta: Bring 8 quarts of water to a boil. Add the salt and raab. Cook for 10 minutes, or until the raab starts to fall apart. Add the pasta to the pot. Cook until the pasta is al dente, then drain well (the raab retains a lot of water), reserving 2 cups of the pasta cooking water. (If using fresh pasta, which takes just 1 to 2 minutes to cook through, cook the raab for about 18 minutes before adding the pasta.)

Make the garlic oil: In a small skillet, place the olive oil, garlic, and red pepper flakes over medium-low heat. Cook, without allowing the garlic to color, for 30 seconds, until aromatic.

To serve: Place the pasta and raab in a large bowl. Stir in the warm garlic oil and Pecorino, thinning out as needed with some of the reserved pasta cooking water. Adjust the seasoning; serve hot.

Cooking with Fennel

Fennel is one of my favorite vegetables, and if my refrigerator is without at least one plump bulb, I feel bereft. I love fennel shaved raw into salads; blanched for a few minutes, then slowly roasted as a side dish; paired with fish or pork; and sautéed in pasta sauces, especially with sausage (see Caramelized Fennel and Crumbled Sausage Sauce, page 117). At the market, look for unblemished, plump, round bulbs; the elongated bulbs are the males and tend to be more bitter. The less prominent the fibers on the outside of the bulb, the better: pronounced fibers mean stringy, fibrous fennel. To prepare fennel, cut off the long stalks atop the bulb; these can be thrown into chicken or fish stock or can be used as a base for roasting meats or fish. The feathery fronds can be washed and chopped and added to any dish, raw or cooked, for extra fennel flavor. Cut off the base of the bulb, then cut the bulb itself in quarters. Remove the white, triangular core from each quarter, then slice or shave the fennel, depending on the recipe; I suggest rinsing the sliced fennel to get rid of latent dirt before using.

Sautéed Zucchini, Herb, and Scallion Sauce

Sugo di Zucchine al Cipollotto ed Erbe This traditional Basilicata combination is even more delectable when Pecorino is added, and egg is stirred into the sauce at the end, creating a sumptuous, creamy dish. SERVES 4

Ingredient notes: The best zucchini are small; avoid large zucchini, which are watery.

WINE PAIRING: CARBONE FIANO BASILICATA

For the pasta:

2 tablespoons salt

1 pound penne rigate or fusilli

For the sauce:

2 tablespoons extra-virgin olive oil
6 scallions (white and tender green parts), thinly sliced
2 pounds small zucchini, cut into ½-inch dice
1 teaspoon salt
2 large eggs
1 cup (¼ pound) freshly grated Pecorino Romano

¼ teaspoon freshly ground black pepper

¼ cup fresh mint leaves, torn or chopped at the last moment
¼ cup fresh basil leaves, torn or chopped at the last moment
1 tablespoon minced fresh oregano

Make the pasta: Bring 5 quarts of water to a boil. Add the salt and the pasta. Cook until the pasta is al dente, then drain, reserving 2 cups of the pasta cooking water.

Meanwhile, make the sauce: In a deep, wide saucepan large enough to accommodate the pasta, place the olive oil and scallions. Warm over medium-high heat for 2 minutes. Add the zucchini and cook for 10 minutes, stirring often, until soft and lightly browned. Season with the salt and keep warm. (The sauce can be made up to this point 2 days in advance; refrigerate until needed, then warm before proceeding.)

In a bowl, beat the eggs with the Pecorino and pepper.

To serve: Transfer the drained pasta to the saucepan. Toss to coat thoroughly with the sauce. Stir in the beaten egg mixture and the mint, basil, and oregano, tossing constantly. Sauté over medium heat for 1 minute, thinning out the sauce as needed with some of the reserved pasta cooking water. Adjust the seasoning and serve hot.

Spicy Chili-Garlic Paste

Sugo Piccante all'Aglio You have to love spicy food to enjoy this easy sauce from Basilicata. The garlic mellows and softens in the oil before being pounded, resulting in a sweet and creamy garlic flavor rather than a pungent one. SERVES 4

Ingredient notes: Seek out dried Italian chili peppers from Calabria; they are easy to find in Italian markets and have amazing flavor.

WINE PAIRING: D'ANGELO VILLA DEI PINI BIANCO

For the pasta:

2 tablespoons salt

1 pound cavatelli or orecchiette

For the sauce:

¼ cup extra-virgin olive oil
5 garlic cloves, 4 peeled and 1 minced

6 hot dried Calabrese chili peppers
1 teaspoon salt

Make the pasta: Bring 5 quarts of water to a boil. Add the salt and the pasta. Cook until the pasta is al dente, then drain, reserving 2 cups of the pasta cooking water.

Meanwhile, make the sauce: In a skillet, place the olive oil, the peeled garlic, and the chilies. Warm over low heat for 5 minutes, until the garlic is fragrant and soft. Do not burn the garlic or chilies, or the sauce will be bitter. Transfer the peeled garlic and chilies to a mortar (leaving the olive oil in the skillet) and pound the garlic and chilies with a pestle until a somewhat smooth paste forms; stir in the salt. If you do not have a mortar and pestle, a small food processor will do, or you can use the back of a large chef's knife to smear the cooked garlic and chilies on a cutting board.

Add the minced garlic to the reserved olive oil in the skillet and cook over medium heat for 30 seconds, until fragrant. Stir in the chili-garlic paste and cook for about 3 minutes, stirring often, until it smells rich and has turned a deeper shade of red. Keep warm.

To serve: Transfer the drained pasta to a deep bowl. Toss vigorously with the warm sauce, thinning out the sauce as needed with some of the reserved pasta cooking water. Adjust the seasoning and serve hot.

Sausage Sauce with Fresh Ricotta

Sugo di Salsiccia e Ricotta Ricotta often replaces cream in central and southern Italy, lending sauces richness without much fat. This sauce from Basilicata takes little time to make, and lends itself to improvisations. SERVES 4

Ingredient notes: Avoid sausages made with vinegar, as it will give the sauce an unpleasant tang.

WINE PAIRING: CANTINE DEL NOTAIO AGLIANICO DEL VULTURE IL REPERTORIO

For the pasta:

2 tablespoons salt

I pound mezzi rigatoni or penne rigate

For the sauce:

I tablespoon extra-virgin olive oil
I pound hot Italian sausages, casings removed and sausages crumbled
4 garlic cloves, minced
I cup water, plus extra as needed

¾ pound fresh whole-milk ricotta cheese
I cup (¼ pound) freshly grated Pecorino Romano
½ teaspoon freshly ground black pepper
Salt as needed

Make the pasta: Bring 5 quarts of water to a boil. Add the salt and the pasta. Cook until the pasta is al dente, then drain, reserving 2 cups of the pasta cooking water.

Meanwhile, make the sauce: In a wide saucepan large enough to accommodate the pasta, place the olive oil and sausage. Cook over medium heat for 8 minutes, or until the sausage is browned; the sausage should be in tiny pieces, so break it up with a spoon as it cooks. Add the garlic and cook for 2 minutes. Add the water and cook for 10 minutes, or until the sausage is tender, adding water as needed. Adjust the seasoning; keep warm. (The sauce can be made up to this point 2 days in advance; refrigerate until needed, then warm gently before proceeding.)

To serve: Transfer the pasta, ricotta, Pecorino, and pepper to the saucepan. Sauté over high heat for 1 minute, thinning out as needed with some of the reserved pasta cooking water. The sauce will look grainy, which is normal. Adjust the seasoning; serve hot.

Calabria

High mountains, rugged coastline, hilltop towns that seem lost in time: the Calabrese landscape is a surprise to most first-time visitors. There are wild boar and wolves in the dense woods, and ancient Greek ruins dot the five-hundred-mile-long coast that stretches along the sea. Since wheat is Calabria's main crop (much of the land is mountainous and hard to cultivate), breads, savory pies called *pitta*, and pasta share pride of place on the family table. Most fresh pastas are made with just semolina flour and water, though some recipes also call for eggs to lend extra suppleness and richness. Sauces vary extensively: some feature just-caught fish and seafood with a bare hint of tomatoes or white wine; others draw out incredible flavor from vegetables and herbs; and still others call for slow-cooking tough cuts of meat to supreme tenderness. Pork is Calabria's favorite meat, so it often ends up in the saucepot in the form of salami, pancetta, guanciale, prosciutto, capocollo, or sausage.

Gently Cooked Red Onion "Jam"

Crema di Cipolle Sweating onions with water for a long time renders them soft enough to crush with a spoon. This pasta is all about the sweetness of the onions and the gentle note of basil. SERVES 4

Ingredient notes: The red onions of Tropea in Calabria are famous in Italy for their sweet taste. Use white onions, which are milder than others, if your red onions have a bite.

WINE PAIRING: LUIGI SCALA CIRÒ ROSATO

For the sauce:

1 ½ pounds sweet red onions, thinly sliced
1 cup water, plus extra as needed
¼ cup extra-virgin olive oil

12 fresh basil leaves, torn
1 teaspoon salt
½ teaspoon freshly ground black pepper

For the pasta:

2 tablespoons salt

1 pound vermicelli, zite, or bucatini

Make the sauce: In a deep, wide saucepan large enough to accommodate the pasta, place the onions. Pour in the water and cover with a tight-fitting lid. Cook over medium heat, stirring occasionally and making sure there is some water in the pan to prevent scorching, for 30 minutes, until the onions are soft and the water has nearly evaporated. You are sweating the onions, not caramelizing them; they should not take on any color. Uncover the pan and cook until all of the water evaporates, stirring vigorously with a wooden spoon the entire time, thereby helping the onions to achieve a soft, creamy consistency. Stir in the olive oil, basil, salt, and pepper. Adjust the seasoning and keep warm. (The sauce can be made up to this point 2 days in advance; refrigerate until needed, then warm gently before proceeding.)

Meanwhile, make the pasta: Bring 5 quarts of water to a boil. Add the salt and the pasta. Cook until the pasta is al dente, then drain, reserving 2 cups of the pasta cooking water.

To serve: Toss the drained pasta with the sauce in the pan and sauté over high heat for 1 minute to meld the flavors, thinning out the sauce as needed with some of the reserved pasta cooking water. Adjust the seasoning and serve hot.

Puréed Sweet Pepper and Tomato Sauce with Basil and Guanciale

Sugo alla Jonica Here's an unusual Calabrese way to incorporate sweet peppers in a pasta sauce. The peppers are first boiled, then puréed along with peeled tomatoes, before sautéing with garlic and guanciale. SERVES 4

Ingredient notes: Don't make this sauce if ripe, fresh tomatoes aren't available: you need their distinctive sweetness.

WINE PAIRING: ODOARDI VIGNA MORTILLA

For the sauce:

1½ pounds ripe, juicy tomatoes, cored
1½ pounds red bell peppers, halved and seeded
¼ cup extra-virgin olive oil
3 garlic cloves, minced

¼ pound guanciale or pancetta, cut into ¼-inch dice
1 teaspoon salt
¼ teaspoon freshly ground black pepper
½ cup water, plus extra as needed

For the pasta:

2 tablespoons salt
1 pound fusilli lunghi, spaghetti, or bucatini

1 cup (¼ pound) freshly grated Pecorino Romano
16 fresh basil leaves, torn

Make the sauce: Bring 2 quarts of water to a boil. Have a large bowl of cool water handy by the pot of boiling water.

Using a paring knife, cut an X into the bottom of each tomato. Drop the tomatoes into the boiling water; cook for about 30 seconds for ripe tomatoes and about 2 minutes for firmer tomatoes, until the skins begin to loosen. Remove the tomatoes with a slotted spoon to the bowl of cool water. After a few minutes, remove the tomatoes from the cool water (reserve the bowl of water). Cut the tomatoes in half crosswise and scoop out the seeds. Finely dice the tomatoes and set aside; collect any of the juices from the cutting board and add them to the diced tomatoes. Reserve the pot of water.

Drop the bell peppers in the reserved water and cook for 5 to 8 minutes, or until soft and pliable; you should be able to peel off the skin (although with some difficulty as compared to the tomatoes). Remove to the bowl of cool water. After a few minutes, drain and peel. Coarsely chop the bell peppers and add to the tomatoes in the bowl.

In the bowl of a food processor, purée the tomatoes and bell peppers until almost smooth.

In a deep, wide saucepan large enough to accommodate the pasta, place 2 tablespoons of the olive oil. Add the garlic and guanciale and set over medium heat. Cook for about 5 minutes, until the guanciale smells rich and has lost its raw look and the fat has been cooked off. Add the puréed tomatoes and peppers and season with the salt and pepper. Pour in the water. Bring to a gentle boil and cover. Reduce the heat to medium-low and cook for about 15 minutes, or until the sauce is rich and the flavors have melded, adding a bit of water as needed to keep a moist consistency. Adjust the seasoning and keep warm. (The sauce can be made up to this point 2 days in advance; refrigerate until needed, then warm gently before proceeding.)

Meanwhile, make the pasta: Bring 5 quarts of water to a boil. Add the salt and the pasta. Cook until the pasta is al dente, then drain, reserving 2 cups of the pasta cooking water.

To serve: Toss the drained pasta with the sauce in the saucepan and stir in the Pecorino, the remaining 2 tablespoons of olive oil, and the basil. Sauté over high heat for 1 minute to meld the flavors, thinning out the sauce as needed with some of the reserved pasta cooking water. Adjust the seasoning and serve hot.

Mom's Roasted Pepper and Olive Sauce

When I was a child, my mom cooked all of our meals. Never complicated, her food was tasty, honest, and seasonal. In the summer, she roasted peppers, and when the peppers were not served as a vegetable dish with olive oil, basil, and garlic, she dropped them into tomato sauce with a handful of olives and a few basil leaves, making a succulent, meaty pasta sauce without any meat at all. Of all the pasta sauces she made, this was one of my favorites. She typically paired this sauce with short pasta, such as penne rigate. When I asked her how she came up with the recipe, she told me that she had eaten it as a child: her family's cook in Milan, a woman named Sandrina who hailed from Emilia, had made it for her, and it had become one of her favorites too. I still make this sauce in my cooking classes and people are always surprised at how easy and delicious it is.

Savory Pork Sauce with Tomatoes and Porcini

Sugo alla Silana In Calabria, guanciale or pancetta, prosciutto, and salami are slow-cooked with juicy tomatoes, dried porcini, and herbs until a redolent sauce forms. The dried porcini are not reconstituted in water before cooking; they are scrubbed to get rid of surface grit, then cooked to tenderness along with the other ingredients, making the dish intensely mushroomy as a result. SERVES 4

Ingredient notes: Caciocavallo is a firm cow's milk cheese with a nutty, sweet flavor and it melts beautifully. If unavailable, aged Provolone will work.

WINE PAIRING: COLACINO VIGNA COLLE BARABBA

For the sauce:

2 tablespoons extra-virgin olive oil

2 garlic cloves, minced

1 tablespoon minced fresh flat-leaf parsley

8 fresh basil leaves, torn

¼ teaspoon red pepper flakes

1 medium yellow onion, minced

1¼ pounds ripe, juicy tomatoes, diced

¾ ounce dried porcini mushrooms, scrubbed with a dry towel to remove surface grit

¼ pound guanciale or pancetta, cut into ¼-inch dice

¼ pound prosciutto di Parma, in one thick slice, cut into ¼-inch dice

¼ pound Italian salami, casings removed, cut into ¼-inch-thick slices, then cut into ¼-inch dice

½ teaspoon salt

¼ teaspoon freshly ground black pepper

½ cup water, plus extra as needed

For the pasta:

2 tablespoons salt

1 pound rigatoni, penne rigate, or mezzi rigatoni

2 tablespoons (¼ stick) unsalted butter

½ cup (2 ounces) coarsely grated young Caciocavallo or Provolone

½ cup (2 ounces) freshly grated Pecorino Romano

Make the sauce: In a deep, wide saucepan large enough to accommodate the pasta, place the olive oil. Add the garlic, parsley, basil, red pepper flakes, and onion. Scatter the tomatoes over the onion and top with the porcini, guanciale, prosciutto, and salami. Season with the salt and black pepper and pour in the water. Cover with a tight-fitting lid and set over medium-low heat. Simmer, stirring occasionally and adding a bit of water as needed to keep a moist consistency, for about 2 hours, or until the tomatoes have thickened nicely and the flavors have formed a rich medley. Adjust the seasoning and keep warm. (The sauce can be made up to this point 2 days in advance; refrigerate until needed, then warm gently before proceeding.)

Meanwhile, make the pasta: Bring 5 quarts of water to a boil. Add the salt and the pasta. Cook until the pasta is al dente, then drain, reserving 2 cups of the pasta cooking water.

To serve: Toss the drained pasta with the sauce, butter, Caciocavallo, and Pecorino in the saucepan. Sauté over high heat for about 1 minute to meld the flavors, or until the cheeses have melted, thinning out the sauce as needed with some of the reserved pasta cooking water. Adjust the seasoning and serve hot.

Mushroom, Cabbage, and Bean Sauce

Millecosedde The Calabrese name of this dish means "a thousand things": a steaming pot of legumes cooked down with mushrooms and cabbage, tossed with boiled pasta. If you are pressed for time and wish to avoid soaking dried beans overnight and then shucking off their skins, or cannot obtain dried cicerchie and fava beans (see Ingredient notes below), you can substitute three 15.5-ounce cans of beans (cannellini, lentils, and chickpeas) instead: rinse and drain the canned beans and slow-cook for 1 hour with the remaining ingredients. This pot of beans is so good that I often make it as a soup (no pasta added at all) and serve it as a main course, accompanied by grilled bread rubbed with a cut garlic clove. SERVES 4

Ingredient notes: If you can find dried fava beans and cicerchie, both add incredible depth to this dish; they are available by mail order and at specialty markets (see page 229). Cicerchie are wild chickpeas, common in southern and central Italy but almost unknown in the north. Remember that dried beans (whole fava beans, cicerchie, and cannellini beans) need to have their tough outer skins removed after soaking; please don't omit this step or the dish will be inedible.

WINE PAIRING: STATTI GAGLIOPPO CALABRIA

For the sauce:

1 ½ ounces dried split fava beans, rinsed and picked over

1 ½ ounces dried cicerchie, rinsed and picked over

1 ½ ounces dried chickpeas, rinsed and picked over

1 ½ ounces dried cannellini beans, rinsed and picked over

1 ½ ounces dried brown or green lentils, rinsed and picked over

3 cups cool water, plus extra as needed

1 medium yellow onion, minced (about ½ cup)

1 celery stalk, minced (about ½ cup)

½ pound savoy cabbage leaves, finely chopped (about 3 cups)

¼ pound button mushrooms, rinsed and minced

2 teaspoons salt

½ teaspoon freshly ground black pepper

2 tablespoons plus ¼ cup extra-virgin olive oil

For the pasta:

2 tablespoons salt

1 pound zite, sedanini, or mezze penne

½ teaspoon red pepper flakes

½ cup (2 ounces) freshly grated Pecorino Romano (optional)

Make the sauce: Soak the dried fava beans, cicerchie, chickpeas, and cannellini beans in cool water to cover overnight. The lentils should *not* be soaked. Discard the soaking water.

Slip the skins off the fava beans if they still have their skins on (this will be the case if using whole instead of split fava beans), the cicerchie, and the cannellini beans. The chickpeas do not need to have their skins removed. In a large pot, place the shucked fava beans, the shucked cicerchie, the chickpeas, and the shucked cannellini beans; add the rinsed lentils (the lentils do not need to be shucked). Pour in 3 cups of cool water and add more if needed to cover the beans completely. Add the onion, celery, cabbage, mushrooms, salt, black pepper, and 2 tablespoons of the olive oil. Set over medium heat and bring to a boil. Reduce the heat to medium-low and cook for about 3 hours, until tender, adding water as needed; the texture should be soupy and thick, not reduced and sauce-like. If you wish, you can crush the beans with the back of a spoon as they cook down, so that the sauce becomes a bit velvety in texture rather than just chunky. Adjust the seasoning and keep warm. (The sauce can be made up to this point 2 days in advance; refrigerate until needed, then warm gently before proceeding.)

Make the pasta: Bring 5 quarts of water to a boil. Add the salt and the pasta. Cook until the pasta is almost but not quite al dente, then drain, reserving 2 cups of the pasta cooking water.

To serve: Add the pasta to the sauce and sauté over high heat for about 4 minutes, or until the pasta is al dente, thinning out the sauce as needed with some of the reserved pasta cooking water and stirring constantly. Stir in the remaining ¼ cup of olive oil and the red pepper flakes. Adjust the seasoning (if the sauce is not salty enough, the flavor will be very bland and beany, so taste for salt before serving and don't be shy). Serve hot, topped with the Pecorino, if you like.

Sicily and Sardinia stand alone in the Mediterranean Sea, and both consider themselves a continent apart from the rest of Italy. Quite distinct from each other, the two islands share little in the kitchen except an abiding love for simple semolina pastas, an abundant use of Pecorino cheese, a reliance on saffron for golden color and subtle aroma, and a generous hand with extra-virgin olive oil. Sardinia's coastline offers fresh seafood and fish that often find their way into pasta sauces, and the game that roams its mountainous inner reaches is slow-cooked to create succulent ragùs. Sicily's centuries of Arab and, later, French dominion have left a palpable imprint on the cuisine, with sweet and savory mingling in one dish and often complex sauces finding their way to the table.

THE ISLANDS

Sicily

The largest island in the Mediterranean, Sicily was dubbed "the Granary of the Empire" by the ancient Romans, thanks to its plentiful wheat cultivation. As a result, bread and pasta are Sicily's mainstays, and the Sicilians have a saying: *Cambia sempre, come la salsa* ("It always changes, like the sauce"). Pasta was often the only dish Sicilian farmers ate in prewar years, and it was tossed with every condiment available: simple tomato sauces, herbs both cultivated and wild, or beaten eggs and cubes of Caciocavallo cheese; when money was scarce, toasted bread crumbs stood in for grated cheese, a custom that persists today despite a much-improved economy. Feast days still bring luxurious pastas, but everyday meals remain far simpler affairs, and most pasta sauces feature seasonal vegetables (eggplant, cauliflower, and tomato are favorites) treated with typical Sicilian exuberance.

Pork Ragù with a Hint of Dark Chocolate and Cinnamon

Sciabbò' di Castrogiovanni Sicilian food can be baroque: several ingredients combine to create a symphonic whole, and there is often an interplay of savory and sweet. This recipe perfectly embodies this colorful spirit. Don't be put off by the touch of dark chocolate in the ragù: it lends a deep, savory note without tasting chocolaty. And don't be tempted to add more cinnamon, as its flavor is meant to be subtle. SERVES 4

Ingredient notes: You'll need good-quality dark chocolate for this dish, with a minimum of 60% cocoa content.

WINE PAIRING: ALESSANDRO DI CAMPOREALE KAID

For the sauce:

2 tablespoons extra-virgin olive oil
1 large yellow onion, very thinly sliced
½ pound pork shoulder, coarsely ground
1 cup dry red wine
¼ cup tomato paste
1 cup water, plus extra as needed

1 teaspoon salt
½ teaspoon freshly ground black pepper
1 teaspoon sugar
⅛ teaspoon ground cinnamon
¾ ounce bittersweet chocolate, finely chopped

For the pasta:

2 tablespoons salt

1 pound reginette or bucatini

Make the sauce: In a saucepan large enough to accommodate the pasta, place the olive oil and onion. Cook over medium heat for about 10 minutes, until the onion releases its aroma and becomes translucent. Add the pork and cook, stirring often to break it into tiny pieces, for about 10 minutes; the pork should look rich and brown and all of the water in the pan should have evaporated. Deglaze with the wine and cook, scraping the bottom of the pan, for about 5 minutes, or until the wine almost fully evaporates. Stir the tomato paste into the water and pour it into the saucepan. Season with the salt and pepper. Cover and reduce the heat to low. Keep at a gentle simmer and cook for 1 hour. Be sure that there is always some liquid in the pan, or the meat will be dry and stringy rather than moist and delicious. (The sauce can be made up to this point 2 days in advance; refrigerate until needed, then warm gently before proceeding.) Stir in the sugar, cinnamon, and chocolate and warm over low heat for about 5 minutes, until the chocolate melts. Adjust the seasoning and keep warm.

Make the pasta: Bring 5 quarts of water to a boil. Add the salt and the pasta. Cook until the pasta is al dente, then drain, reserving 2 cups of the pasta cooking water.

To serve: Toss the drained pasta into the sauce. Sauté over high heat for 1 minute to meld the flavors, thinning out the sauce as needed with some of the reserved pasta cooking water. Adjust the seasoning and serve hot.

Italy's Favorite Nuts

Pine nuts (pignoli in Italian) are surely the nut most associated with Italian cooking: stirred into sauces for fish or meat, ground into countless pestos, and used in desserts from the north to the islands, pine nuts have long been a staple in Italian cooking, especially in the savory cooking of Sicily. Pine nuts from Italy are elongated and slightly tapered; those from Pisa are most prized. They are more buttery in flavor than their Chinese counterparts, and are available (at a steep price) from Italian specialty markets. Chinese pine nuts can be distinguished because they have a telltale triangular shape and a dark area at the tapered end. Like all nuts, pine nuts are high in fats and should be stored in the freezer to maintain freshness.

Fried Eggplant Sauce with Tomatoes and Ricotta Salata

Sugo alla Norma This dish is typical of Catania and is the very essence of summer. If you don't like frying, brush the eggplant slices with 2 tablespoons of olive oil and roast them in a preheated oven at 350°F for about 30 minutes. I coarsely chop the fried eggplant slices before serving, so every bite gets a mouthful, but the presentation is more striking (and traditional) with whole eggplant slices. SERVES 4

Ingredient notes: Look for small Italian eggplant or pale mauve Sicilian eggplant at specialty markets or farm stands; regular eggplant will work, but the flavor will be more bitter.

WINE PAIRING: CALEA NERO D'AVOLA

For the sauce:

2 pounds small eggplant (preferably Italian or Sicilian)
1 tablespoon plus 1 teaspoon salt
2 pounds ripe, juicy tomatoes, cored

½ cup plus 1 tablespoon extra-virgin olive oil
2 garlic cloves, minced
32 fresh basil leaves, torn
½ teaspoon freshly ground black pepper

For the pasta:

2 tablespoons salt
1 pound spaghetti or strozzapreti

1 cup (¼ pound) freshly grated ricotta salata cheese, plus extra for passing at the table

Make the sauce: Using a vegetable peeler, remove long, thin strips of peel from the top to the bottom of the eggplant, leaving some skin attached; the eggplant will look striped (removing some of the peel will help keep the eggplant in whole slices after frying). Cut the eggplant into ½-inch-thick slices. Place the eggplant slices in a colander over a plate and sprinkle with 1 tablespoon of the salt; set aside for 1 hour to purge their bitter juices. Blot dry.

Meanwhile, using a paring knife, cut an X into the bottom of each tomato. Bring 1 quart of water to a boil and drop in the tomatoes; cook for about 30 seconds for ripe tomatoes and about 2 minutes for firmer tomatoes, until the skins begin to loosen. Drain the tomatoes. Place them in a large bowl of cool water for 5 minutes, then drain them and slip off the skins. Cut the tomatoes in half crosswise and scoop out the seeds. Finely dice the tomatoes and set aside; collect any juices from the cutting board and add them to the diced tomatoes.

In a deep, wide skillet, place ¼ cup of the olive oil over medium heat. Heat for about 1 minute, until the oil begins to shimmer but not smoke. Add as many of the eggplant slices as will fit in a single layer and cook, for about 4 minutes per side, turning once, until golden on both sides and soft all the way through. Remove to a tray lined with paper towels and blot dry. Add ¼ cup of the olive oil to the skillet, warm it again until shimmering, and fry the remaining eggplant slices in the same way.

In a saucepan large enough to accommodate the pasta, place the remaining tablespoon of olive oil. Add the garlic and warm gently over medium heat for about 30 seconds, until aromatic; the garlic can take on a bit of golden color. Add half of the basil and all of the tomatoes, season with the remaining teaspoon of salt and the pepper, and bring to a boil. Cover and cook for 15 minutes, adding a bit of water if needed. (The sauce can be made up to this point 2 days in advance; refrigerate until needed, then warm gently before proceeding.) Adjust the seasoning and keep warm.

Make the pasta: Bring 5 quarts of water to a boil. Add the salt and the pasta. Cook until the pasta is al dente, then drain, reserving 2 cups of the pasta cooking water.

To serve: Toss the drained pasta, ricotta salata, and the remaining basil with the warm tomato sauce. Sauté over high heat for 1 minute to meld the flavors, thinning out the sauce as needed with some of the reserved pasta cooking water. Adjust the seasoning and serve hot, topped with the fried eggplant slices and additional ricotta salata.

Almond-Tomato Pesto from Trapani

Pesto Trapanese Pesto need not be about basil: it is a sauce made by pounding herbs (*pestare* in Italian, hence the name), with or without nuts and garlic, in a mortar. Making pesto in the bowl of a food processor or blender yields a smoother sauce with less old-fashioned charm, but it certainly speeds up the process. SERVES 4

> **Ingredient notes:** Sicilians use blanched almonds for this pesto, which have a lighter flavor and color than skin-on almonds, but I prefer the latter for their more intense, nutty taste. Store nuts in the freezer, as their high fat content makes them prone to rancidity.

WINE PAIRING: RIOFAVARA ELORO SPACCAFORNO

For the sauce:

½ cup unflavored bread crumbs, such as panko (optional)

2 ounces skin-on almonds

1 pound ripe, juicy tomatoes, cored

6 garlic cloves, peeled

16 fresh basil leaves

1 teaspoon salt

½ teaspoon freshly ground black pepper

¼ cup extra-virgin olive oil

For the pasta:

2 tablespoons salt

1 pound bucatini or spaghetti

Make the sauce: If using bread crumbs, place the bread crumbs in a small dry skillet and heat gently over medium heat, stirring often, for about 5 minutes, until the bread crumbs turn a shade darker and are aromatic; be careful not to burn them. Transfer to a bowl and set aside.

Place the almonds in the bowl of a food processor and pulse a few times until they are the size of very coarse meal or tiny peas; they should not be pulverized. Transfer to the same skillet in which you cooked the bread crumbs and cook the almonds over medium heat for about 3 minutes, stirring often, until they turn a golden color and smell toasty; be careful not to burn them. Remove to another bowl.

Bring 1 quart of water to a boil. Have a large bowl of cool water handy by the pot of boiling water. Using a paring knife, cut an X into the bottom of each tomato. Drop the tomatoes into the boiling water; cook for about 30 seconds for ripe tomatoes and about 2 minutes for firmer tomatoes, until the skins begin to loosen. Drain the tomatoes. Place them in the bowl of cool water for 5 minutes, then drain them and slip off the skins. Cut the tomatoes in half crosswise and scoop out the seeds. Finely dice the tomatoes and set aside; collect any of the juices from the cutting board and add them to the diced tomatoes.

In the bowl of a food processor (or blender if you do not have a food processor), place the seeded and peeled tomatoes, the garlic, basil, salt, and pepper. Pulse a few times, then, while the motor is running, gradually pour in the olive oil to create a somewhat smooth sauce. Transfer to a deep, large bowl that will accommodate the pasta and stir in the chopped toasted almonds. Adjust the seasoning. If you are not about to serve the pasta within minutes, lay plastic wrap directly on top of the pesto to prevent darkening. (The sauce can be made up to this point 2 days in advance; refrigerate until needed, then bring to room temperature before proceeding.)

Make the pasta: Bring 5 quarts of water to a boil. Add the salt and the pasta. Cook until the pasta is al dente, then drain, reserving 2 cups of the pasta cooking water.

To serve: Stir the pasta into the pesto in the serving bowl, thinning out the sauce as needed with some of the reserved pasta cooking water. Adjust the seasoning and serve hot, topped with the toasted bread crumbs, if you like.

Roasted Pepper Sauce with Eggplant, Tomatoes, and Olives

Sugo alla Siracusana This sauce is bold, vibrant, summery. There is the salty note of capers and olives, the mellow sweetness of roasted peppers and tomatoes, the pleasant bite of eggplant, and, of course, the fragrance of basil at the end. SERVES 4

Ingredient notes: Sicilians prefer their capers packed in salt; the flavor is saltier, and purely that of caper, not at all briny. Be sure to rinse salt-packed capers, and chop finely if they are large.

WINE PAIRING: MANENTI CERASUOLO DI VITTORIA

For the sauce:

¾ pound small eggplant (preferably Italian or Sicilian), peel on, cut into ½-inch cubes

1 tablespoon plus ½ teaspoon salt

1 pound ripe, juicy tomatoes, cored

1 large, fleshy yellow bell pepper, halved and seeded

3 tablespoons extra-virgin olive oil

4 oil-packed anchovy fillets, drained, or 2 salted anchovies, boned, gutted, and rinsed

2 garlic cloves, minced

½ cup pitted black olives, chopped

2 tablespoons salted capers, rinsed and drained, or capers in brine, drained (chopped if large)

20 fresh basil leaves, torn

½ teaspoon freshly ground black pepper

1 cup water, plus extra as needed

For the pasta:

2 tablespoons salt

1 pound zite or spaghetti

1 cup (¼ pound) freshly grated aged Caciocavallo or Pecorino Romano, plus extra for passing at the table

Make the sauce: In a colander over a plate, place the eggplant cubes and sprinkle with 1 tablespoon of the salt; set aside for 1 hour to purge their bitter juices. Squeeze dry.

Meanwhile, make the sauce: Bring 1 quart of water to a boil. Have a large bowl of cool water handy by the pot of boiling water. Using a paring knife, cut an X into the bottom of each tomato. Drop the tomatoes into the boiling water; cook for about 30 seconds for ripe tomatoes and about 2 minutes for firmer tomatoes, until the skins begin to loosen. Drain the tomatoes. Place them in the bowl of cool water for 5 minutes, then drain them and slip off the skins. Cut the tomatoes in half crosswise and scoop out the seeds. Finely dice the tomatoes and set aside; collect any of the juices from the cutting board and add them to the diced tomatoes.

Preheat the broiler.

Line a rimmed baking sheet with aluminum foil. Place the halved and seeded bell pepper on the foil, cut side down. Slip under the preheated broiler and broil for about 12 minutes, or until the skin is blistered and black. Wrap in the aluminum foil and allow to steam until cool enough to handle. Peel off the skin and cut the peeled roasted pepper into ¼-inch-wide strips, then into ¼-inch dice.

In a deep, wide saucepan large enough to accommodate the pasta, place the olive oil and the anchovies. Warm gently over medium heat for about 1 minute, until the anchovies break down to a paste, crushing them with a fork or spoon to help them break down. Add the garlic and cook for about 30 seconds, or until aromatic, then stir in the eggplant and cook, stirring as needed, for about 5 minutes, until golden all over and soft almost all the way through. Stir in the tomatoes and diced roasted pepper and cook for 5 minutes. Add the olives, capers, and half of the basil; season with the remaining ½ teaspoon of salt and the pepper, and pour in the water. Bring to a boil. Cover and cook for 10 minutes, adding a bit of water as needed to maintain a moist consistency. Adjust the seasoning and keep warm. (The sauce can be made up to this point 2 days in advance; refrigerate until needed, then warm gently before proceeding.)

Meanwhile, make the pasta: Bring 5 quarts of water to a boil. Add the salt and the pasta. Cook until the pasta is al dente, then drain, reserving 2 cups of the pasta cooking water.

To serve: Toss the drained pasta with the sauce. Stir in the Caciocavallo and the remaining basil and sauté over high heat for 1 minute to meld the flavors, thinning out the sauce as needed with some of the reserved pasta cooking water. Adjust the seasoning and serve hot, topped with additional Caciocavallo.

Sardinia

A mysterious island, Sardinia feels very much like it is cut off from the mainland; in fact, Sardinians refer to the rest of Italy as "the Continent." Inhabited continuously since the Neolithic era, Sardinia has been invaded and settled by very diverse cultures, but it is the Spanish who left the biggest imprint on the local cuisine. The island's most characteristic pasta is malloreddus: short, saffron-tinted gnocchi made from just semolina and water, best savored with hearty meat sauces. Another favorite pasta shape is maccheroni al ferretto, short spaghetti shaped around a knitting needle, usually paired with light tomato sauces or seafood preparations. Pasta sauces vary across the island, with wild boar or hare ragùs popular in the wooded areas, chunky seafood sautés common along the sea, and simple concoctions everywhere else, like sausage with tomatoes, or saffron and ricotta cheese, or toasted bread crumbs with parsley.

Red Mullet Roe with Garlicky Bread Crumbs

Sugo di Bottarga Sardinian cuisine relies more on the fruits of the land than on those of the sea: since the Neolithic era, people largely settled inland, away from potential seafaring invaders. Today there are elegant resort towns, as well as a number of ancient cities, along the sea. Bottarga, Sardinia's gray mullet "caviar," is often the star of pasta sauces; here, it marries with garlic-scented toasted bread crumbs to create a subtle marine flavor. SERVES 4

Ingredient notes: Bottarga is made from the salted and pressed eggs of large fish; in Sardinia, gray mullet is used. Do not buy pre-grated bottarga, as the flavor is less intense. You will need to peel away the paper-thin outer membrane from the bottarga before grating it.

WINE PAIRING: PIERO MANCINI VERMENTINO DI SARDEGNA

For the pasta:

2 tablespoons plus ¼ teaspoon salt

1 pound malloreddus or spaghetti

For the bread crumbs:

2 tablespoons plus ¼ cup extra-virgin olive oil
3 garlic cloves, halved
2 ounces unflavored bread crumbs, such as panko
½ teaspoon salt
½ teaspoon freshly ground black pepper

3 ounces gray mullet bottarga, thin outer membrane peeled, finely grated

Make the pasta: Bring 5 quarts of water to a boil. Add the salt and the pasta. Cook until the pasta is al dente, then drain, reserving 2 cups of the pasta cooking water.

Meanwhile, make the bread crumbs: In a small skillet, place 2 tablespoons of the olive oil and the garlic. Warm gently over medium heat for about 5 minutes, until infused. Press with the back of a spoon on the garlic cloves to further release their aroma, then discard the garlic cloves. Add the bread crumbs, season with ¼ teaspoon of the salt and ¼ teaspoon of the pepper, and heat gently over medium heat, stirring often, for about 5 minutes, until the bread crumbs turn golden and are aromatic; be careful not to burn the bread crumbs.

To serve: In a wide, shallow bowl, place the grated bottarga. Add the drained pasta, the remaining ¼ cup of olive oil, the remaining ¼ teaspoon of salt, and the remaining ¼ teaspoon of pepper. Thin out the sauce as needed with some of the reserved pasta cooking water. Adjust the seasoning (bottarga can be quite salty, so be careful), and serve hot, topped with the bread crumbs.

Cooking in Terra-Cotta

Earthenware pots—known as *terra cotta* in Italy—are one of the oldest and most wonderful cooking vessels. Across Italy, but especially in the south, cooks have often used sturdy, heavy-walled terra-cotta pots to slow-cook tough cuts of meat, sometimes sealing the top with a sort of gluey dough made from flour and water if a lid wasn't handy; the aromas of the stew within intensified and moisture was perfectly maintained, yielding tender, fall-off-the-bone meat hours later. Some pasta sauces, notably long-simmered bean sauces and ragùs, are ideal cooked in terra-cotta. If the pot is large enough, you can add the pasta to it after draining and bring the whole assembly to the table for a dramatic presentation. Just make sure when buying your terra-cotta pots that they are intended for cooking rather than for decorative purposes. Terra-cotta pots need to be seasoned (soaked in water for twenty-four hours before the first use), and a flame tamer may be a good idea to prevent cracking due to extreme temperature changes.

Dried Porcini Mushroom Sauce with Cream, Garlic, and Chili

Sugo ai Funghi Porcini Secchi con Panna The Sardinian woods are home to mushrooms of all sorts; porcini are served fresh in spring and fall, then dried for use throughout the year. For this savory sauce, they are cooked with garlic and a hint of chili pepper and finished with a splash of cream. SERVES 4

> **Ingredient notes:** The best dried porcini are meaty and large, and they look very much like mushrooms, stems, caps, and all; select dried porcini that are as large as possible, not crumbled and broken.

WINE PAIRING: MANDROLISAI ROSSO SUPERIORE

For the sauce:

2 ounces dried porcini mushrooms	¼ teaspoon red pepper flakes
2 cups cool water, plus extra as needed	½ cup heavy cream
1 tablespoon extra-virgin olive oil	1 teaspoon salt
3 garlic cloves, minced	¼ teaspoon freshly ground black pepper

For the pasta:

2 tablespoons salt	2 tablespoons minced fresh flat-leaf parsley
1 pound malloreddus, cavatelli, or cheese ravioli	

Make the sauce: Place the dried porcini in a bowl and pour in the 2 cups of water; if this is not enough to cover, add more water as needed. Set aside for about 1 hour, or until plump and soft. Drain the porcini, reserving the soaking liquid. Rinse and coarsely chop the porcini and set aside. Strain the soaking liquid through a sieve lined with paper towels or cheese-cloth to get rid of the grit that usually comes off the dried porcini. Reserve the strained soaking liquid.

In a saucepan large enough to accommodate the pasta, place the olive oil, garlic, and red pepper flakes. Cook over medium heat for about 1 minute, until the garlic releases its aroma, being careful not to burn the garlic or it will take on a bitter flavor. Add the chopped porcini and sauté for 10 minutes, adding as much of the reserved, strained soaking liquid as needed to keep about ½ cup of liquid in the pan at all times. Stir in the cream, salt, and black pepper and bring to a gentle boil. Adjust the seasoning as needed. Keep warm. (The sauce can be made up to this point 2 days in advance; refrigerate until needed, then warm gently before proceeding.)

Make the pasta: Bring 5 quarts of water to a boil. Add the salt and the pasta. Cook until the pasta is al dente, then drain, reserving 2 cups of the pasta cooking water.

To serve: Toss the drained pasta into the sauce. Stir in the parsley and sauté over high heat for 1 minute to meld the flavors, thinning out the sauce as needed with some of the reserved pasta cooking water. Adjust the seasoning and serve hot.

Cooking with Dried Porcini Mushrooms

Dried mushrooms—like sundried tomatoes, or dried chili peppers—have a charm and a use all their own. They are not a substitute for fresh mushrooms, but rather, an entirely different product that can lend exceptional depth and meatiness to any dish. For Italian cooking, and particularly for intensely flavored pasta sauces, the best choice is dried porcini mushrooms; they are often labeled *cepes* (their French name). Italian markets carry a good selection, but do check the label to ensure that you are buying genuine porcini from Italy, as opposed to cheaper varieties from other countries (most commonly, China and Croatia). When buying dried porcini mushrooms, look for those with the most intact mushroom shape and the largest caps. Soak in cool water (rather than hot, which robs the mushrooms of their flavor) and save the soaking water (pass it through a colander lined with paper towels or a coffee filter to get rid of grit) to lend extra richness to the sauce or to soups, risottos, and even sauces for meat. Dried porcini keep for a year in a cool, dry, dark pantry.

Lamb Ragù with Sun-Dried Tomatoes and Saffron

Ragù di Agnello con Pomodori Secchi In this recipe, lamb shoulder is simmered with basil, sun-dried tomatoes, and white wine, making for a ragù with complex flavor and a hint of sweetness. The use of saffron is typical of Sardinian cooking. **SERVES 4**

Ingredient notes: Lamb shoulder has the correct fat content to yield a succulent ragù; avoid loin, which is too lean and makes for a rubbery, flavorless ragù.

WINE PAIRING: ARGIOLAS COSTERA CANNONAU DI SARDEGNA

For the sauce:

2 tablespoons extra-virgin olive oil

1 large yellow onion, minced (about 1 cup)

2 garlic cloves, minced

¾ pound lamb shoulder, cut into ¼-inch dice

½ cup dry white wine

½ cup sun-dried tomatoes packed in olive oil, drained and minced

16 fresh basil leaves, torn

½ teaspoon saffron threads

¾ pound ripe tomatoes, cut into ½-inch dice

1 cup chicken stock or water, plus extra as needed

1 teaspoon salt

½ teaspoon freshly ground black pepper, plus extra for serving

For the pasta:

2 tablespoons salt

1 pound malloreddus or cavatelli

1 cup (¼ pound) freshly grated Pecorino Sardo or Pecorino Romano

Make the sauce: In a saucepan large enough to accommodate the pasta, place the olive oil, onion, and garlic. Cook over medium heat for about 10 minutes, until the onion releases its aroma and becomes translucent. Add the lamb and cook, stirring often, for about 10 minutes; the meat should look rich and brown and any liquid in the pan should have evaporated. Add the wine and cook for about 2 minutes, until it nearly evaporates, scraping the bottom of the pan to release any bits of meat that are clinging to it. Stir in the sun-dried tomatoes, basil, saffron, tomatoes, and stock. Season with the salt and pepper. Cover and reduce the heat to low. Simmer gently for 1 ½ to 2 hours, or until the lamb is very tender. Be sure that there is always about ½ cup of liquid in the pan, or the meat will be dry and stringy rather than moist and delicious; add stock as needed. Adjust the seasoning as needed. Keep warm. (The sauce can be made up to this point 2 days in advance; refrigerate until needed, then warm gently before proceeding.)

Make the pasta: Bring 5 quarts of water to a boil. Add the salt and the pasta. Cook until the pasta is al dente, then drain, reserving 2 cups of the pasta cooking water.

To serve: Toss the drained pasta into the sauce. Stir in the Pecorino and sauté over high heat for 1 minute to meld the flavors, thinning out the sauce as needed with some of the reserved pasta cooking water. Adjust the seasoning, sprinkle with pepper, and serve hot.

Saffron in Italian Cooking

Saffron is a long-standing crop in Sardinia, Abruzzo, and the Marches; Tuscany and Latium have recently started cultivating saffron. So across Italy, saffron pistils provide both a subtle color and warming flavor to pasta sauces. Most recipes suggest infusing or steeping the saffron in boiling liquid (usually wine or cream), but in Sardinia, cooks usually toast saffron in a dry skillet before adding it to the liquid in a dish, thereby intensifying its aroma. The Sardinians make a delicious and quick sauce by toasting saffron in a hot skillet until aromatic, then mixing it into creamy fresh Ricotta and letting it sit while they boil the pasta; a drizzle of olive oil is added along with pasta cooking water to think out the ricotta-saffron sauce, and the dish is ready. When selecting saffron, choose whole pistils, preferably those with a deep red (rather than orange) color; powdered saffron is often stretched with less costly annatto or turmeric. Saffron can only be picked by hand, and it takes approximately 150 *crocus sativus* flowers to yield just 1 gram of saffron, which explains why saffron is such an expensive spice.

Rich Lobster Sauce

Sugo all'Aragosta Lobster is a staple in Alghero (a town with a profound Catalan influence) and Bosa (a colorful hamlet with a stunning view of the Sardinian countryside). In this recipe, lobster chunks are simmered in a light tomato sauce; the water in which the lobsters are cooked is reserved for boiling the pasta later, adding a briny marine depth to the final dish. SERVES 4

Ingredient notes: If you buy lobsters already cooked, make sure they are cooked just hours before serving.

WINE PAIRING: SELLA & MOSCA THILION

For the sauce:

2 tablespoons plus 1 teaspoon salt
2 medium live lobsters (1½ pounds each)
2 pounds ripe tomatoes, cored
¼ cup extra-virgin olive oil
2 garlic cloves, minced

1 tablespoon minced fresh flat-leaf parsley
8 fresh basil leaves, torn
½ teaspoon freshly ground black pepper, plus
    extra for serving

For the pasta:

1 pound spaghetti or bucatini

Make the sauce: Bring 10 quarts of water to a rolling boil in a very deep pot; it needs to be deep enough to hold both lobsters easily. Add 2 tablespoons of the salt and drop in the lobsters headfirst. Cover the pot and cook for 8 minutes. Remove the lobsters to a tray and cool to room temperature. Reserve the lobster cooking water. The lobsters will not be fully cooked and will finish cooking in the sauce later.

Pick the lobster meat out of the tail shell and cut into large chunks. Crack the claws with a meat mallet or nutcracker to facilitate extracting the meat and pull out the claw meat as well; cut into large chunks.

Return the lobster water to a boil. Have a large bowl of cool water handy by the pot of boiling water. Using a paring knife, cut an X into the bottom of each tomato. Drop the tomatoes into the boiling water; cook for about 30 seconds for ripe tomatoes and about 2 minutes for firmer tomatoes, until the skins begin to loosen. Remove the tomatoes using a slotted spoon. Place the tomatoes in the bowl of cool water for 5 minutes, then drain them and slip off the skins. Cut the tomatoes in half crosswise and scoop out the seeds. Finely dice the tomatoes and set aside; collect any of the juices from the cutting board and add them to the diced tomatoes. Reserve the pot of boiling water.

In a saucepan large enough to accommodate the pasta, place 2 tablespoons of the olive oil, the garlic, parsley, and basil. Cook over medium heat for about 1 minute, or until the garlic is aromatic; be careful not to burn the garlic. Add the tomatoes, the remaining teaspoon of salt, and the pepper and bring to a boil. Reduce the heat to medium-low; cover and simmer for 15 minutes, adding a bit of water as needed to maintain a moist consistency. Stir in the lobster chunks and return to a gentle boil. Simmer for about 5 minutes, or until the aroma is rich and deep. Adjust the salt if needed. Keep warm.

Make the pasta: Return the lobster water to a boil. Add the pasta. Cook until the pasta is al dente, then drain, reserving 2 cups of the pasta cooking water.

To serve: Toss the pasta with the sauce and sauté over high heat for 1 minute to meld the flavors, thinning out the sauce as needed with some of the reserved pasta cooking water. Adjust the seasoning, drizzle with the remaining 2 tablespoons of olive oil, sprinkle with pepper, and serve hot.

Basic Recipes

The recipes in this chapter are the backbone of many well-loved dishes and, once mastered, will serve you well for years to come. The best thing about these recipes is that, like much of Italian cooking, they are simple to prepare and deliver amazing flavor—as long as the ingredients you choose are of impeccable quality.

- Fresh Tomato Sauce
- Fresh Egg Pasta
- Rustic Semolina Flour Pasta (Without Egg)
- Light-as-Air Ricotta Gnocchi
- Mom's Foolproof Potato Gnocchi

Fresh Tomato Sauce

Sugo di Pomodoro Fresco There are almost as many ways to make tomato sauce in Italy as there are cooks. Some recipes start with carrots, onions, celery, and perhaps a bit of garlic. Others add a garlic clove still in its skin, to be plucked out after it releases its fragrance into the sauce (Italians call this *aglio in camicia,* or garlic with a shirt). Many opt for passing the tomatoes through a food mill for a super-smooth consistency. I love the natural texture of chopped fresh tomatoes, and I usually just dice fresh, ripe tomatoes, skipping the peeling and seeding step described below—in the latter case, what results is a chunky sauce with bits of skin and seeds, and a deeper flavor with a touch more acidity, since the seeds are quite flavorful. If you skip the peeling and seeding step, the sauce takes about 5 minutes to prepare. MAKES ABOUT 6 CUPS TOMATO SAUCE (ENOUGH FOR 1½ POUNDS PASTA)

Ingredient notes: I prefer small, juicy tomatoes (often labeled Campari tomatoes in the United States) for this sauce, but ripe plum tomatoes, or even beeftsteaks, work beautifully too. Campari tomatoes tend to be very sweet and juicy, even in the winter. In the cool months, if you cannot find a truly good, ripe tomato, I suggest canned San Marzano tomatoes, which hail from the Campania region of Italy and have the perfect balance of sweetness and acidity and a mellow, delicate taste. Just be sure they are the real thing from Italy, and not a domestic version: cans of authentic San Marzano tomatoes sport a distinct DOP symbol (Denominazione di Origine Protetta [Protected Designation of Origin]).

3 pounds ripe tomatoes
¼ cup extra-virgin olive oil

12 fresh basil leaves, cut into fine strips or torn into pieces
1½ teaspoons salt
⅛ teaspoon freshly ground black pepper

If you are skipping the peeling and seeding step, then simply remove the stem end from each tomato and dice the tomatoes into ½-inch cubes.

If you wish to peel and seed the tomatoes for the sauce, bring 4 quarts of water to a boil. Have a large bowl of cool water handy by the pot of boiling water. Using a paring knife, cut an X into the bottom of each tomato. Drop the tomatoes into the boiling water; cook for about 30 seconds for ripe tomatoes and about 2 minutes for firmer tomatoes, until the skins begin to loosen. Drain the tomatoes. Place them in the bowl of cool water for 5 minutes, then drain them and slip off the skins. Cut the tomatoes in half crosswise and scoop out the seeds. Finely dice the tomatoes and set aside; collect any of the juices from the cutting board and add them to the diced tomatoes.

In a 3-quart saucepan, place 2 tablespoons of the olive oil and half of the basil. Warm gently over a low heat for about 1 minute, just until the basil starts to become fragrant. Add the tomatoes and any of their juices, the salt, and the pepper. Bring to a gentle boil. Cover and reduce the heat to medium-low; simmer for 25 minutes. Stir in the remaining 2 tablespoons of olive oil and the remaining half of the basil. Taste and adjust the seasoning. The sauce can be frozen for up to 2 months, or refrigerated for up to 1 week.

A Word About Tomato Sauce

As you cook from this book, you'll find that none of the tomato-based recipes call for tomato paste or sugar. The reason is simple: I prefer the clean taste of tomatoes to shine through. I find that adding tomato paste or tomato concentrate makes for a jammy sauce that overwhelms both the pasta and the other ingredients in the sauce. I also find that good-quality tomatoes (whether fresh, ripe tomatoes or canned San Marzano tomatoes) have the correct balance of sweet and acid; adding sugar throws off this balance and makes the sauce unnaturally sweet to my palate. And you'll notice that my Fresh Tomato Sauce (see page 221) and my tomato-based vegetable sauces are not simmered too long; usually 30 minutes or less is enough to align the flavors in a tomato-based sauce (unless meat is added, as for ragù, but that is a whole other type of sauce where slow, lengthy cooking brings out different flavors in its constituent ingredients). By cooking a tomato sauce for hours, you mute its direct, lively flavor, its lovely freshness . . . and isn't that freshness, that lovely taste of summer, why we all crave tomato sauce in the first place?

Fresh Egg Pasta

Pasta Fresca all'Uovo This recipe is for classic wheat flour and egg pasta, which is silky and delicate. My favorite fresh egg pasta is made with half un-bleached all-purpose flour and half semolina flour; the semolina provides a hearty, toothsome texture. Make the classic dough below a few times to get com-fortable working the dough, then try variations with different flour combinations and different amounts of egg, water, or white wine. If you would like to add flavor-ings to your pasta dough, remember to add any wet ingredients (such as puréed chopped spinach, tomato paste, beet purée, squid ink) to the egg (and add a bit more flour to compensate for the extra moisture) and add any dry ingredients (such as dried porcini mushroom powder, black pepper, cayenne pepper) to the flour. **MAKES 1½ POUNDS FRESH PASTA**

Ingredient notes: The standard ratio for the classic egg pasta is 3½ ounces of flour (about ¾ cup) for every large egg. Of course, different types of flour absorb more or less liquid; higher-protein flours (such as King Arthur) may require a bit of extra water to come together, whereas low-protein flours (such as White Lily) will seem very wet and require additional flour.

3¼ cups (14 ounces) unbleached all-purpose flour, plus extra for the counter and trays (or half each unbleached all-purpose flour and semolina flour)

¼ teaspoon salt
4 large eggs
Semolina flour for dusting

Make the pasta dough: Place the flour and salt on a counter; mix thoroughly. Make a well in the center and add the eggs to the well. Using a fork at first, beat the eggs as you would for scrambled eggs. Then begin to draw the flour into the eggs little by little. When most of the flour has been incorporated, begin kneading the dough by hand; knead for about 10 min-utes, until it is smooth and firm and all of the flour has been incorporated. If the dough is dry, add a touch of cool water (do this slowly: 1 teaspoon of water will make a much bigger difference than you might imagine!); if it is moist, add a touch of flour (again, do this gingerly: add only as much as needed to prevent sticking, as you do not want to make a dry dough).

To check if the dough is ready, cut it in half; when ready, there should be tiny air bubbles present, almost as if the dough contained yeast, and the color should be even throughout. There should be no bits of unincorporated flour. If it is not ready, knead longer.

Shape into a ball, dust with flour, and place under an inverted bowl or wrap in plastic wrap. Let rest for 30 minutes to relax the gluten, which makes rolling out easier.

When you are ready to roll out the dough, cut the pasta dough into 4 pieces. Working with 1 piece at a time and keeping the others covered to prevent drying out, roll out each piece into a thin sheet using a pasta machine. I suggest you run each piece through the lowest setting of the machine first (the setting with the rollers farthest apart) at least three or four times to develop elasticity and finish kneading the dough. Then roll each piece through each successive setting once, sprinkling with semolina flour each time to prevent sticking. On most pasta machines, 9 is the highest setting and results in very thin sheets of pasta. Depending on the sauce I am making and the way I am cutting my pasta (such as tagliatelle, spaghetti, linguine, or pappardelle), I don't always go to the thinnest setting. Thinner pasta is ideal for delicate or smooth sauces, thicker pasta for heartier, chunky sauces.

Once the sheets have been rolled out, lay them on a semolina-dusted counter and cut them into 8-inch-long pieces. Let rest for 10 to 20 minutes, to let them dry a bit so they can be properly cut. Flip the pieces once during the drying time and dust both sides with semolina. If you do not dry the pasta at all before rolling it through the cutters of the pasta machine, the resulting strands will stick together. If you dry the pasta too long and it begins to crack, the resulting strands will break into short lengths. How long you need to dry the sheets prior to cutting depends on how moist the dough is, how humid it is in the kitchen, and how thick the sheets are (thicker sheets require longer drying).

Sprinkle each sheet generously with semolina flour and pass through the cutting attachment of your pasta machine. Most machines come with a spaghettini and a tagliatelle attachment. Or, to cut by hand, dust generously with semolina flour and loosely roll up each piece jelly roll–style, then cut into ⅛-inch-wide strips (or wider if desired). Toss with semolina flour to prevent sticking. Spread out in a single layer on several semolina-dusted trays until ready to use. This pasta will cook through very quickly if it is fresh when cooked: 1 to 2 minutes after it hits the boiling water.

The dough can be made up to 2 days ahead and refrigerated. The rolled-out pasta can be refrigerated on several trays for up to 2 days, or frozen up to 1 month. When cooking frozen pasta, transfer it straight from the freezer into boiling water without defrosting first.

Rustic Semolina Flour Pasta (Without Egg)

Pasta Fresca Senza Uova This is the dough for cavatelli, orecchiette, fusilli al ferretto, and all manner of southern Italian pastas. It is harder to work than egg pasta because it isn't as elastic, but it is well worth the effort. I often use it to make short tagliatelle that pair splendidly with chunky vegetable sauces (especially broccoli raab, broccoli, or asparagus). **MAKES 1½ POUNDS FRESH PASTA**

> **Ingredient notes:** Semolina flour is made from coarsely milled durum wheat and has a golden color and sweet flavor. It is available at health food markets and Italian food stores.

3¼ cups (14 ounces) semolina flour, plus extra for the counter and trays

¼ teaspoon salt

Place the semolina on the counter and mix in the salt. Make a well in the center and add enough hot water to make a dough that comes together; it will take about 1 cup of water. The dough should be firm and form a solid mass. Add more water if the dough is ragged and does not come together (keep in mind that this dough should be quite firm, almost hard).

Knead vigorously for 5 to 10 minutes, or until very smooth. Any graininess should be completely gone. If the dough is still grainy, knead longer. Shape into a ball, dust with flour, and place under an inverted bowl or wrap in plastic wrap. Let rest for 30 minutes to relax the gluten, which makes rolling out easier.

To make tagliatelle or spaghetti (most pasta machines come with a spaghettini and a tagliatelle attachment): Cut the pasta dough into 4 pieces. Working with 1 piece at a time and keeping the others covered to prevent drying out, roll out each piece into a thin sheet using a pasta machine. I suggest you run each piece through the lowest setting of the machine first (the setting with the rollers farthest apart) at least 3 or 4 times to develop elasticity and finish kneading the dough. Then roll each piece through each successive setting once, sprinkling with semolina flour each time to prevent sticking. On most pasta machines, 9 is the highest setting and results in very thin sheets of pasta. Depending on the sauce I am making and the way I am cutting my pasta (such as tagliatelle, spaghetti, linguine, or pappardelle), I don't always go all the way to the thinnest setting. Thinner pasta is ideal for delicate or smooth sauces, thicker pasta for heartier, chunky sauces.

Once the sheets have been rolled out, lay them on a semolina-dusted counter and cut them into 8-inch-long pieces. Let rest for 10 to 20 minutes, to let them dry a bit so they can be properly cut. Flip the pieces once during the drying time and dust both sides with semolina. If you do not dry the pasta at all before rolling it through the cutters of the pasta machine, the resulting strands will stick together. If you dry the pasta too long and it begins to crack, the resulting strands will break into short lengths. How long you need to dry the sheets prior to cutting depends on how moist the dough is, how humid it is in the kitchen, and how thick the sheets are (thicker sheets require longer drying).

Sprinkle each sheet generously with semolina flour and pass them through the cutting attachment of your pasta machine. Or, to cut by hand, dust generously with semolina flour and loosely roll up each piece jelly roll–style, then cut into ⅛-inch-wide strips (or wider if desired). Toss with semolina flour to prevent sticking. Spread out in a single layer on several semolina-dusted trays until ready to use. This pasta will cook through quickly if it is fresh when cooked: about 2 minutes after it hits the boiling water.

To make cavatelli, which can be done easily with a cavatelli machine available from a number of online retailers: Cut the dough into 20 pieces, roll each into a log, and cover with a towel. Roll through the cavatelli machine and toss amply with semolina flour to prevent sticking. Cavatelli will take about 6 minutes to cook through after it hits the boiling water.

The dough can be made up to 2 days ahead and refrigerated. The rolled-out pasta can be refrigerated on several trays for up to 2 days, or frozen up to 1 month. When cooking frozen pasta, transfer it straight from the freezer into boiling water without defrosting first.

Light-as-Air Ricotta Gnocchi

Gnocchi di Ricotta If you are looking for a recipe that makes you look like a genius but only takes moments of work, this is it: you can make a batch of gnocchi within minutes, and the results are delicious every time. You can add snipped chives and caraway seeds for an Alpine flavor (delicious with sage butter sauce) or minced parsley and sage for color (excellent with tomato- or meat-based sauces). **MAKES 1½ POUNDS FRESH GNOCCHI**

Ingredient notes: If possible, buy fresh ricotta from a cheese shop, as opposed to tubs of ricotta from the supermarket shelf. Supermarket ricotta is too wet and will require too much flour to hold it together, resulting in heavy gnocchi. If you cannot find fresh ricotta, place super-market ricotta in a sieve set over a bowl and allow it to drain for a few hours.

1 pound fresh whole-milk ricotta cheese
½ cup (2 ounces) freshly grated Pecorino Romano
½ teaspoon salt

¼ teaspoon freshly ground black pepper
1 cup (4½ ounces) unbleached all-purpose flour,
   plus extra for the counter and trays

In a large bowl, place the ricotta, Pecorino, salt, and pepper. Stir with a spoon. Add the flour; stir until a dough forms; the mixture should hold together when rolled in your hands.

If the dough is sticky, add a bit more flour. Do not add too much flour or the gnocchi will be dry and heavy. This dough is not meant to be kneaded, so it should be a bit soft and tacky. If you knead the dough, it will require additional flour and the gnocchi will be heavy.

Gather the dough with your hands into a mass and dust with flour. Cut into 10 pieces and roll each piece into a ½-inch-thick log. Cut each log into ½-inch pieces using a dough scraper and toss with flour. Arrange in a single layer on several flour-dusted trays.

Before cutting and shaping all the gnocchi, test the gnocchi by dropping a few in boiling water; add more flour if the gnocchi are too wet or fall apart, but be careful: the more flour you add, the heavier the gnocchi will be. If they are firm, work in a bit of water.

The uncooked gnocchi will hold in the refrigerator 24 hours spread out on trays, dusted with flour to prevent sticking, and covered with a towel or plastic wrap.

Mom's Foolproof Potato Gnocchi

Gnocchi di Patate della Mamma This is my mom's recipe and it works every time—provided, of course, that you weigh the ingredients instead of eyeballing them. Whatever you do, do not put the potatoes through a food processor or they will turn into a gluey mess; use a potato ricer (it looks like a big garlic press).

MAKES 1½ POUNDS FRESH GNOCCHI

Ingredient notes: I prefer Yukon Gold potatoes, which yield sweeter gnocchi; some cooks like russet potatoes, which make for starchier gnocchi. Do not use baby potatoes.

18 ounces Yukon Gold potatoes, skin on, scrubbed
½ teaspoon salt
¼ teaspoon freshly ground black pepper (optional)

1 cup plus 2 tablespoons (5 ounces) unbleached all-purpose flour, plus extra for the counter and trays

In a 4-quart pot, place the potatoes and cover with cold water. Bring to a boil over high heat and cook for about 30 minutes, until the potatoes are tender when pierced with a knife.

Drain and peel the potatoes; pass them through a potato ricer onto a counter. Allow to cool to room temperature. (If you make the gnocchi while the potatoes are warm, the potatoes will "sweat" and require additional flour, making for heavy gnocchi.)

Add the salt and pepper (if using) to the potatoes and mix well. Sprinkle the flour over the potatoes and mix until smooth. If the dough is sticky, add a bit more flour. Do not add too much flour or the gnocchi will be heavy. This dough is not meant to be kneaded, so it should be a bit soft. If you knead it, it will require additional flour and the gnocchi will be heavy.

Gather the dough with your hands into a mass and dust with flour. Cut into 10 pieces and roll each piece into a ½-inch-thick log. Cut each log into ½-inch pieces using a dough scraper and toss with flour. Arrange in a single layer on several flour-dusted trays.

Before cutting and shaping all the gnocchi, test the gnocchi by dropping a few in boiling water; add more flour if the gnocchi are wet or fall apart, but be careful: the more flour you add, the heavier the gnocchi will be. If they are too firm, work in a bit of water.

The uncooked gnocchi will hold in the refrigerator 24 hours spread out on trays, dusted with flour to prevent sticking, and covered with a towel or plastic wrap.

Mail-Order Sources

Most of the stores and importers listed here will ship anywhere in the country with sufficient notice. A few do not provide mail-order services, but they are included because they have such a good selection that they are worth mentioning for those who can visit them in person.

A. G. Ferrari Foods

3490 Catalina Street
San Leandro, CA 94577
(877) 878-2783
www.agferrari.com
An impressive array of dried goods, olive oils, condiments, tomato products, and more.

Agata & Valentina

1505 First Avenue
New York, NY 10021
(212) 452-0690
www.agatavalentina.com
Selection of pastas, cheeses, cured meats, and more.

Amazon.com

For cicerchie (wild chickpeas) as well as many other hard-to-find delicacies.

BuonItalia

75 Ninth Avenue
New York, NY 10011
(212) 633-9090
www.buonitalia.com
Fresh, dried, and frozen pastas include trofie, malloreddus, fregola, pizzoccheri, garganelli, and cavatelli. A great selection of Italian cheeses, imported Italian chili peppers (I love their Calabrese hot peppers), and olive oils as well.

Dean & Deluca

121 Prince Street
New York, NY 10012
(800) 221-7714
www.deandeluca.com
Nearly every grain, type of flour, and pasta is available, as are many hard-to-find cheeses, bottarga, cured meats, game, fowl, and more.

DiBruno Brothers House of Cheese
930 South Ninth Street
Philadelphia, PA 19147
(215) 922-2876
(888) 322-4337
www.dibruno.com
Italian cheeses, an array of dried pastas, and specialty products.

Esposito's Pork Shop
354 West Thirty-Eighth Street
New York, NY 10018
(212) 279-3298
www.espositosausage.com
Homemade Italian pork sausages, as well as game, fowl, and specialty meats on special order.

Fantes Kitchen Shop
1006 S. Ninth Street
Philadelphia, PA 19147-4798
(215) 922-5557
(800) 443-2683
www.fantes.com
An addictive website where you can buy everything you'll ever need for fresh pasta making (and general cooking and baking).

Formaggio Kitchen
244 Huron Avenue
Cambridge, MA 02138
(617) 354-4750
(888) 212-3224
www.formaggiokitchen.com
This shop carries an incredible selection of Italian cheeses, as well as dried pastas, olive oils, and more.

Gotham Wines & Liquors
2517 Broadway
New York, NY 10025
(212) 932-0990
www.gothamwines.com
Excellent selection of Italian (and world) wines and spirits, at hard-to-beat prices.

Melissa's World Variety Produce
P.O. Box 514599
Los Angeles, CA 90021
(800) 588-0151
www.melissas.com
Common and unusual fruits and vegetables.

Penzeys, Limited, Spices and Seasonings
12001 W. Capitol Drive
Wauwatosa, WI 53222
(262) 785-7676
(800) 741-7787
www.penzeys.com
Unbelievable selection of herbs, spices, and extracts.

Acknowledgments

Writing a cookbook, testing recipes, and styling photographs, all the while running a cooking school and teaching, is not easy—it's a lot of fun, and immensely gratifying, but it's hard to find the necessary hours in the day to get it all done. I could not possibly have done this properly if it were not for two amazing people: Gerry Biordi and Elizabeth Simms. Ever since we opened Rustico Cooking in 2004, Gerry has been right there alongside us, teaching daily, imparting knowledge with passion, growing with the business, taking on more and more responsibilities with ever more commitment and skill. Elizabeth Simms joined us just a year later; over the last eight years, Elizabeth has grown immensely as a teacher, a chef, and a friend, and I am so proud to rely on her talents and dedication. Without Gerry and Elizabeth, Rustico Cooking would not be what it is today, and I am profoundly grateful for their presence in my life.

I want to thank Caitlyn Nies, who has earned her stripes with flying colors over the last three years teaching and doing a wonderful job with our clients; Melissa Ricketts, aka the Salt Shaker Lady, for being such a joy to work with; Lauren Wilson, Anthony Contrino, Nora Watson, and Sunny Gandara, wonderful teachers at our school; and Gyula Halasz and Szabina Domokos, for being such an important part of our team over the last five years.

In the process of writing the book and getting it into its final production stages, I want to thank Costas Mouzouras above all. Costas has long been my wine guru, a commensurate source of all wine-related knowledge. And with this book, he took on the daunting task of providing an ideal wine pairing for each of the eighty recipes and he kept the regional flavor of my dishes intact through his pairings.

I am indebted to Judith Riven, my agent and friend; she has always been able to spot a book idea in its infancy stage, and she is unparalleled in her efficiency and dedication.

At Ballantine Books, I owe a debt of gratitude to Pamela Cannon, my editor, for her keen eye and editorial input, and for allowing me to maintain my culinary voice. To Betsy Wilson, who has been of the utmost help throughout each step of the editorial process, always with a gracious attitude. And to Liz Cosgrove and Joe Perez for doing such a beautiful job with the layout, design, and cover of the book.

Closer to home, I want to thank Doug and Grazina Crisman, and Lou and Joan Malacrida, for being wonderful neighbors and friends, and for allowing us to pilfer their flatware, napkins, and more as we styled the photos in the book.

My parents have always been my biggest supporters; they never questioned my choices, even when I changed course several times early on; they have always given me their unconditional love, and for this I will be forever grateful.

And there are no words to express how deeply thankful I am each and every day to be sharing my life with the most amazing man: my husband, Dino De Angelis, who over the years became my business partner; he is my life's companion, my inspiration, and my best friend. He is also the incredibly talented photographer responsible for the book's images, a self-taught artist of many media who never fails to amaze me with his creativity.

Index

Abruzzo, 88, 101, 125, 130–42, 217
Almond-Tomato Pesto from Trapani, 204–5
anchovies, 18, 34, 109, 165
  Quick and Fiery Tomato Sauce with Olives, Capers, and Anchovies, 136, 172–74
  Tuna, Anchovy, and Olive Sauce with Fresh Tomatoes, 96–97, 136
Apulia, 130, 142, 154–64
Artichoke Sauce with White Wine and Porcini Mushrooms, 30–32
arugula, 154, 178
  Spicy Cannellini Bean Sauce with Pancetta and Arugula, 143–45
Asiago, 21
asparagus, xvi, 225
  Crushed Asparagus Sauce, xiii, xv, 136, 151–53
  Sausage, Tomato, and Asparagus Sauce, 114–16

bacon, 53, 121, 144
  Spring Sauce of Fava Beans, Scallions, and Bacon, 127–29
basic recipes, 220–28

basil:
  Creamy Tomato Sauce with Speck, Nutmeg, and Basil, 53–55
  Genoese Basil Pesto, 23–25
  Puréed Sweet Pepper and Tomato Sauce with Basil and Guanciale, 190–92
  Summer Tomato Sauce with Basil and Lemon, 136, 166–68
Basilicata, 101, 130, 178–86
beans, xiii–xvi, 70
  canned, 37, 143, 162
  dried, xv, 37, 135, 143, 162, 195
  Mushroom, Cabbage, and Bean Sauce, 195–96
  Slow-Cooked Cranberry Bean Sauce with Scallions, Pancetta, and Garlic-Parsley Garnish, 36–38, 136
  Spring Sauce of Fava Beans, Scallions, and Bacon, 127–29
beef:
  Mom's Beef Ragù, 42–43
  Slow-Cooked Beef Cheek Ragù, 59–60
brandy:
  Brandied Pork and Mushroom Sauce, 56–57

  Crab Sauce with Saffron and Brandy, 72–73
bread crumbs, 70, 176
  Oven-Roasted Tomato and Bread Crumb Sauce, 157–59
  "Poor Man's" Garlic Bread Crumb Sauce, xv, 175–77
  Red Mullet Roe with Garlicky Bread Crumbs, 210–12
broccoli, xvi, 225
  Garlic-Laced Broccoli Sauce, 136, 146–48
broccoli raab, xvi, 130, 154, 178, 225
  Silky Broccoli Raab, Garlic, and Crushed Red Pepper Sauce, xv, 179–81
butter, 11
  sage, 7, 38, 227
  Warm Poppy Seed Butter with Smoked Ricotta, 64–65

cabbage:
  Mushroom, Cabbage, and Bean Sauce, 195–96
  Sausage and Cabbage Sauce, 91–93
  Slow-Cooked Savoy Cabbage Sauce with Pork, 6–7

cabbage (*cont.*):
  Wilted Cabbage, Potato, and
    Mountain Cheese Sauce,
    39–41
Caciocavallo, 21
Calabria, 101, 130, 185, 187–96
Campania, 130, 165–77
cannellini beans, 195
  Spicy Cannellini Bean Sauce
    with Pancetta and Arugula,
    143–45
central Italy, 4, 89–129
cheese, 11, 21, 70, 92
  and pasta sauces in Italian
    kitchen, xv–xvi
  Wilted Cabbage, Potato, and
    Mountain Cheese Sauce,
    39–41
chicken, xii, 8, 69
  Quick-Cooked Chicken and
    Marsala Sauce, 13–15
chickpeas, xiii, 135
  Chunky Chickpea Sauce, 136,
    162–64
  wild (cicerchie), 136, 149–50,
    195–96
  Wild Chickpea Purée with
    Garlic-Chili Oil, 136, 149–50
clams, 34, 131, 142, 169
  White Clam Sauce, 155–56
cockles, 155–56, 169–71
cooking, 34
  with dried porcini mushrooms,
    214
  of pasta, x–xi, xiii–xvi, 11, 24
  saffron in, 217
  starting cold, olive oil and, 32
  in terra-cotta, 212
  with wine, 54
Crab Sauce with Saffron and
    Brandy, 72–73

eggplants, 198
  Fried Eggplant Sauce with
    Tomatoes and Ricotta
    Salata, 201–3

  Roasted Pepper Sauce with
    Eggplant, Tomatoes, and
    Olives, 136, 206–8
eggs:
  Egg, Sausage, and Guanciale
    Sauce with Lemon and
    Nutmeg, 112–13
  Fresh Egg Pasta, 223–24
  Roman Sauce of Eggs,
    Pancetta, and Parmigiano,
    112–13, 120, 121–23
  Sautéed Zucchini, Herb, and
    Scallion Sauce, 113, 182–84
Emilia-Romagna, 1, 43, 78–88
essential ingredients, 152

fava beans, xvi, 195–96
  Spring Sauce of Fava Beans,
    Scallions, and Bacon, 127–29
fennel:
  Caramelized Fennel and
    Crumbled Sausage Sauce,
    117–19, 180
  cooking with, 180
fennel seeds, 88, 99
fish:
  in Ligurian cooking, 34
  and pasta sauces in Italian
    kitchen, xvi
  serving pasta and, xii–xiv
flour, viii, xv, 34, 40, 223–24, 227
  see also semolina flour
Fontina, 2, 7, 11, 40
  Creamy Fontina Sauce with
    Crushed Walnuts and White
    Truffle Oil, 3–5
  Potato, Onion, and Fontina
    Sauce with Pancetta, 20–21
Friuli-Venezia Giulia, 1, 52, 58–67

garlic, 70
  Dried Porcini Mushroom Sauce
    with Cream, Garlic, and
    Chili, 213–15
  Fragrant Garlic and Parsley
    Sauce, 102–3, 136

  Garlic, Oil, and Chili Pepper,
    168
  Garlic-Laced Broccoli Sauce,
    136, 146–48
  "Poor Man's" Garlic Bread
    Crumb Sauce, xv, 175–77
  Red Mullet Roe with Garlicky
    Bread Crumbs, 210–12
  Sautéed Mushroom Sauce with
    Garlic, Parsley, and Cream,
    10–11
  Shrimp Sauce with Garlic and
    Parsley, 94–95
  Silky Broccoli Raab, Garlic, and
    Crushed Red Pepper Sauce,
    xv, 179–81
  Silky Garlic-Tomato Sauce,
    100–101
  Slow-Cooked Cranberry
    Bean Sauce with Scallions,
    Pancetta, and Garlic-Parsley
    Garnish, 36–38, 136
  Spicy Chili-Garlic Paste,
    185–86
  Wild Chickpea Purée with
    Garlic-Chili Oil, 136, 149–50
gnocchi:
  drooling, 7
  Light-as-Air Ricotta Gnocchi,
    227
  Mom's Foolproof Potato
    Gnocchi, 228
Gorgonzola, 35
  Mom's Creamy Gorgonzola
    Sauce, 44–45
Grana Padano, 21, 35
Grouper Sauce with Olives,
    Aromatic Herbs, and
    Tomatoes, 66–67
guanciale:
  Egg, Sausage, and Guanciale
    Sauce with Lemon and
    Nutmeg, 112–13
  Puréed Sweet Pepper and
    Tomato Sauce with Basil and
    Guanciale, 190–92

Spicy Tomato, Onion, and
Guanciale Sauce, xiv, 124–25

herbs, 187, 193, 198, 204
Crushed Hazelnut and Herb
Sauce, 17–19, 113
Grouper Sauce with Olives,
Aromatic Herbs, and
Tomatoes, 66–67
preserving fresh, 61
Sautéed Zucchini, Herb, and
Scallion Sauce, 113, 182–84

islands, 197–219

lamb:
Lamb Ragù with Sun-Dried
Tomatoes and Saffron,
216–17
Sweet Pepper and Lamb Ragù
with Rosemary, 132–33
Latium, viii, 89, 120–29, 217
lemon, lemon juice, 34
Egg, Sausage, and Guanciale
Sauce with Lemon and
Nutmeg, 112–13
Summer Tomato Sauce with
Basil and Lemon, 136,
166–68
lentils, xiii, 162, 195–96
Simple Lentil Sauce, 134–36
Liguria, 1, 12, 22–34, 101
lobster, 34
Rich Lobster Sauce, 218–19
Lombardy, 1, 22, 35–45, 97

Marches, the, 89–98, 217
Marsala:
Quick-Cooked Chicken and
Marsala Sauce, 13–15
Romagna-Style Ragù with
Marsala and Crispy
Prosciutto, 82–83
marscapone, 21, 35
meats, xv
browning of, 116

finishing pasta and, 70
serving pasta and, xii–xiii
tenderness of, 60
milk, 1–3, 12, 16, 20, 43–44, 46,
62, 79, 82, 89, 113, 116,
120, 131, 193
Slow-Cooked Sausage Ragù
with Milk and a Hint of
Tomatoes, 86–88
Molise, 88, 101, 130, 142–53
Montasio, 21
mushrooms, 53
Artichoke Sauce with
White Wine and Porcini
Mushrooms, 30–32
Brandied Pork and Mushroom
Sauce, 56–57
Dried Porcini Mushroom Sauce
with Cream, Garlic, and
Chili, 213–15
Hunter-Style Sauce with
Mushrooms and Smoked
Prosciutto, 47–49
Mushroom, Cabbage, and
Bean Sauce, 195–96
Sautéed Mushroom Sauce with
Garlic, Parsley, and Cream,
10–11
see also porcini mushrooms
mussels, 34, 130–31, 142, 155
Classic Seafood Sauce, 169–71

northern Italy, 1–88, 101, 160
nutmeg, ix, 46, 88, 92
Creamy Tomato Sauce with
Speck, Nutmeg, and Basil,
53–55
Egg, Sausage, and Guanciale
Sauce with Lemon and
Nutmeg, 112–13
Parmigiano Sauce with Fresh
Nutmeg, 16, 92
nuts, ix, xv
Creamy Fontina Sauce with
Crushed Walnuts and White
Truffle Oil, 3–5

Crushed Hazelnut and Herb
Sauce, 17–19, 113
Pine Nut and Marjoram Pesto,
26–27
pine nuts, 200

olive oil, 70
extra-virgin, xvi, 28–29, 61, 89,
103, 152, 197
Garlic, Oil, and Chili Pepper,
168
and pasta sauces in Italian
kitchen, xv–xvi
Smashed Potato Sauce with
Cracked Black Pepper and
Olive Oil, xv, 98
Starting cold and, 32
tuna in, 96–97
Wild Chickpea Purée with
Garlic-Chili Oil, 136, 149–50
olives, 165
Grouper Sauce with Olives,
Aromatic Herbs, and
Tomatoes, 66–67
Mom's Roasted Pepper and
Olive Sauce, 192
Quick and Fiery Tomato Sauce
with Olives, Capers, and
Anchovies, 136, 172–74
Roasted Pepper Sauce with
Eggplant, Tomatoes, and
Olives, 136, 206–8
Tuna, Anchovy, and Olive
Sauce with Fresh Tomatoes,
96–97, 136
onions:
Caramelized Radicchio and
Onion Sauce, 76–77
Gently Cooked Red Onion
"Jam," 188–90
Potato, Onion, and Fontina
Sauce with Pancetta, 20–21
Spicy Tomato, Onion, and
Guanciale Sauce, xiv,
124–25
taming strong flavor of, 129

pancetta:
    Potato, Onion, and Fontina
        Sauce with Pancetta, 20–21
    Roman Sauce of Eggs,
        Pancetta, and Parmigiano,
        112–13, 120, 121–23
    Slow-Cooked Cranberry
        Bean Sauce with Scallions,
        Pancetta, and Garlic-Parsley
        Garnish, 36–38, 136
    Spicy Cannellini Bean Sauce
        with Pancetta and Arugula,
        143–45
    Sweet Pea and Pancetta Sauce
        for the Feast of San Zeno,
        74–75
Parmigiano-Reggiano, 21
    Parmigiano Sauce with Fresh
        Nutmeg, 16, 92
    Prosciutto di Parma and
        Parmigiano Sauce, xv,
        84–85, 92
    Roman Sauce of Eggs,
        Pancetta, and Parmigiano,
        112–13, 120, 121–23
    saving rinds of, 43
parsley, 70
    Fragrant Garlic and Parsley
        Sauce, 102–3, 136
    Sautéed Mushroom Sauce with
        Garlic, Parsley, and Cream,
        10–11
    Shrimp Sauce with Garlic and
        Parsley, 94–95
    Slow-Cooked Cranberry
        Bean Sauce with Scallions,
        Pancetta, and Garlic-Parsley
        Garnish, 36–38, 136
pasta:
    al dente, xi, xiii, 11
    al forno, 11
    cooking of, x–xi, xiii–xvi, 24
    elegant presentation of, 92
    finishing of, 92
    freshly-made, 152
    history of, viii–ix, xii

imported Italian, 152
in Italian kitchen, xv–xvi
rinsing of, xi, xiii
at room temperature, 136
saucing of, xiii–xvi, 11
serving of, xii–xiv
shapes of, viii, xiv
sweet, 52
texture of, x, xvi, 175
whole wheat, 122
peas, xvi, 114
    Sweet Pea and Pancetta Sauce
        for the Feast of San Zeno,
        74–75
Pecorino and Cracked Black
    Pepper Sauce, 92, 120, 126
pepper (bell), 154
    Mom's Roasted Pepper and
        Olive Sauce, 192
    Puréed Sweet Pepper and
        Tomato Sauce with Basil and
        Guanciale, 190–92
    Roasted Pepper Sauce with
        Eggplant, Tomatoes, and
        Olives, 136, 206–8
    Sweet Pepper and Lamb Ragù
        with Rosemary, 132–33
Pepper (black):
    Pecorino and Cracked Black
        Pepper Sauce, 92, 120, 126
    Smashed Potato Sauce with
        Cracked Black Pepper and
        Olive Oil, xv, 98
pepper (chili), 38, 70, 112
    Dried Porcini Mushroom Sauce
        with Cream, Garlic, and
        Chili, 213–15
    Garlic, Oil, and Chili Pepper,
        168
    Silky Broccoli Raab, Garlic, and
        Crushed Red Pepper Sauce,
        xv, 179–81
    Spicy Chili-Garlic Paste,
        185–86
    Wild Chickpea Purée with
        Garlic-Chili Oil, 136, 149–50

pestos, 22, 101, 200
    Almond-Tomato Pesto from
        Trapani, 204–5
    Genoese Basil Pesto, 23–25
    Pine Nut and Marjoram Pesto,
        26–27
Piave, 21
Piedmont, 1–2, 4, 7, 12–21, 88,
    97, 101
pine nuts, 200
    Pine Nut and Marjoram Pesto,
        26–27
pizzoccheri (buckwheat
    tagliatelle), 39–41
poppy seeds, ix, 52
    Warm Poppy Seed Butter with
        Smoked Ricotta, 64–65
porcini mushrooms, 10, 22,
    223
    Artichoke Sauce with
        White Wine and Porcini
        Mushrooms, 30–32
    Dried Porcini Mushroom Sauce
        with Cream, Garlic, and
        Chili, 213–15
    Savory Pork Sauce with
        Tomatoes and Porcini,
        193–94
pork:
    Brandied Pork and Mushroom
        Sauce, 56–57
    Pork Ragù with a Hint of Dark
        Chocolate and Cinnamon,
        199–200
    Savory Pork Sauce with
        Tomatoes and Porcini,
        193–94
    Slow-Cooked Savoy Cabbage
        Sauce with Pork, 6–7
    Smoked Pork Sauce with
        Chives, 50–52, 113
    Venetian-Style Two-Meat
        Ragù, 69–71
potatoes, xvi
    Mom's Foolproof Potato
        Gnocchi, 228

Potato, Onion, and Fontina
  Sauce with Pancetta, 20–21
Smashed Potato Sauce with
  Cracked Black Pepper and
  Olive Oil, xv, 98
Wilted Cabbage, Potato, and
  Mountain Cheese Sauce,
  39–41
prosciutto:
  di Parma, xv, 53, 78, 84–85,
    92, 140–41, 193
  Fresh Ricotta Sauce with Diced
    Prosciutto, 140–41
  Hunter-Style Sauce with
    Mushrooms and Smoked
    Prosciutto, 47–49
  Prosciutto di Parma and
    Parmigiano Sauce, xv,
    84–85, 92
  Romagna-Style Ragù with
    Marsala and Crispy
    Prosciutto, 82–83
provalone, 21

ragùs, xiv, 11
  Classic Bolognese Ragù,
    79–81
  The Hunter's Rabbit Ragù,
    8–9
  Lamb Ragù with Sun-Dried
    Tomatoes and Saffron,
    216–17
  Mom's Beef Ragù, 42–43
  Pork Ragù with a Hint of Dark
    Chocolate and Cinnamon,
    199–200
  Romagna-Style Ragù with
    Marsala and Crispy
    Prosciutto, 82–83
  Slow-Cooked Beef Cheek
    Ragù, 59–60
  Slow-Cooked Sausage Ragù
    with Milk and a Hint of
    Tomatoes, 86–88
  Sweet Pepper and Lamb Ragù
    with Rosemary, 132–33

Venetian-Style Two-Meat
  Ragù, 69–71
Wild Boar Ragù, 104–6
red mullet, 33–34
  Red Mullet Roe with Garlicky
    Bread Crumbs, 210–12
red snapper, 66
  Delicate Tomato Sauce with
    Diced Red Snapper, 33–34
ricotta:
  Fresh Ricotta Sauce with Diced
    Prosciutto, 140–41
  Light-as-Air Ricotta Gnocchi,
    227
  Sausage Sauce with Fresh
    Ricotta, 186
ricotta salata, 21
  Fried Eggplant Sauce with
    Tomatoes and Ricotta
    Salata, 201–3
  Warm Poppy Seed Butter with
    Smoked Ricotta, 64–65
rosemary, 12–14, 61, 99, 104,
    135
  Sweet Pepper and Lamb Ragù
    with Rosemary, 132–33

saffron, 131, 197, 209
  Crab Sauce with Saffron and
    Brandy, 72–73
  in Italian cooking, 217
  Lamb Ragù with Sun-Dried
    Tomatoes and Saffron,
    216–17
sage, 61, 99
  butter, 7, 38, 227
Salami Sauce Quick-Stewed in
    White Wine, 62–63
salt:
  in cooking pasta, x, 24
  sea, 24, 61, 152
Sardinia, 197, 209–19
sauces, saucing:
  cooking pasta and, x–xi, xiii–xiv
  eggs in, 113
  in history, viii–ix

in Italian kitchen, xv–xvi
of pasta, xiii–xvi, 11
serving pasta and, xii–xiv
sausage, 61, 178, 187, 209
  Caramelized Fennel and
    Crumbled Sausage Sauce,
    117–19, 180
  Egg, Sausage, and Guanciale
    Sauce with Lemon and
    Nutmeg, 112–13
  Italian Sausage: Does it Even
    Exist?, 88
  Sausage, Tomato, and
    Asparagus Sauce, 114–16
  Sausage and Cabbage Sauce,
    91–93
  Sausage Sauce with Fresh
    Ricotta, 186
  Slow-Cooked Sausage Ragù
    with Milk and a Hint of
    tomatoes, 86–88
scallions, 51
  Sautéed Zucchini, Herb, and
    Scallion Sauce, 113, 182–84
  Slow-Cooked Cranberry
    Bean Sauce with Scallions,
    Pancetta, and Garlic-Parsley
    Garnish, 36–38, 136
  Spring Sauce of Fava Beans,
    Scallions, and Bacon, 127–29
Scamorza, 21
seafood:
  Classic Seafood Sauce, 169–71
  finishing pasta and, 70
  in Ligurian cooking, 34
  and pasta sauces in Italian
    kitchen, xv–xvi
semolina flour, 154, 187, 197,
    209, 223–26
  Rustic Semolina Flour Pasta
    (without Egg), 225–26
shrimp, xii
  Classic Seafood Sauce, 169–71
  Shrimp Sauce with Garlic and
    Parsley, 94–95
Sicily, viii, xii, 70, 197–208

southern Italy, xii, 70, 88, 130–96, 225
sugar, ix, 52, 64, 74, 222
Sunday Braciole Sauce, 160–61

tagliatelle, xiv, 74–75, 84–85, 90, 116, 224–25
buckwheat, 39–41
terra-cotta, cooking in, 212
tomatoes, ix
Almond-Tomato Pesto from Trapani, 204–5
canned, 91, 107, 152
freshness of, 191, 221–22
Fried Eggplant Sauce with Tomatoes and Ricotta Salata, 201–3
Grouper Sauce with Olives, Aromatic Herbs, and Tomatoes, 66–67
Lamb Ragù with Sun-Dried Tomatoes and Saffron, 216–17
peeling and seeding of, 221–22
Roasted Pepper Sauce with Eggplant, Tomatoes, and Olives, 136, 206–8
San Marzano, 152, 165, 221–22
Savory Pork Sauce with Tomatoes and Porcini, 193–94
Slow-Cooked Sausage Ragù with Milk and a Hint of Tomato, 86–88
Spicy Tomato, Onion, and Guanciale Sauce, xiv, 124–25
sun-dried, xvi, 216–17
Tuna, Anchovy, and Olive Sauce with Fresh Tomatoes, 96–97, 136

tomato sauce, 70
Creamy Tomato Sauce with Speck, Nutmeg, and Basil, 53–55
Delicate Tomato Sauce with Diced Red Snapper, 33–34
Fresh Tomato Sauce, 30, 33, 36, 53, 69, 82, 169, 172, 221–22
Oven-Roasted Tomato and Bread Crumb Sauce, 157–59
Puréed Sweet Pepper and Tomato Sauce with Basil and Guanciale, 190–92
Quick and Fiery Tomato Sauce with Olives, Capers, and Anchovies, 136, 172–74
Sausage, Tomato, and Asparagus Sauce, 114–16
Silky Garlic-Tomato Sauce, 100–101
Summer Tomato Sauce with Basil and Lemon, 136, 166–68
without tomato paste or sugar, 222
Tomato Sauce with Tiny Meatballs Teramo-Style, 137–39
Trentino-Alto Adige, 1, 46–57
truffles, 17
Aphrodisiac properties, 4
black, 88, 109–11
Black Truffle Sauce in the Style of Spoleto, 110–11
Creamy Fontina Sauce with Crushed Walnuts and White Truffle Oil, 3–5, 113
Tuna, Anchovy, and Olive Sauce with Fresh Tomatoes, 96–97, 136

Tuscany, viii, 22, 88–90, 99–108, 217

Umbria, viii, 4, 88–89, 109–19, 135

Val d'Aosta, 1–11, 20
veal, 59, 79, 82, 99
Mom's Veal Roast Sauce, 14
vegetables:
pasta al forno and, 11
and pasta sauces in Italian kitchen, xv–xvi
serving pasta and, xii–xiii
vegetarians, xii–xiii, 17
"False" Meat Sauce with Red Wine, 107–8
Veneto, the, 1, 68–77, 88

walnuts, 22, 52
Creamy Fontina Sauce with Crushed Walnuts and White Truffle Oil, 3–5, 113
water, 187, 209, 223
in cooking pasta, x–xi, xiii–xvi, 24
serving pasta and, xiii–xiv
wheat, viii, 40, 187, 198, 223
see also semolina flour
whole wheat pasta, 122
Wild Boar Ragù, 104–6
wine, 54
Artichoke Sauce with White Wine and Porcini Mushrooms, 30–32
"False" Meat Sauce with Red Wine, 107–8
Salami Sauce Quick-Stewed in White Wine, 62–63

About the Author

A native of Milan, Italy, MICOL NEGRIN is the owner of Rustico Cooking, an Italian cooking school in Manhattan. She is the author of the James Beard–nominated *Rustico: Regional Italian Country Cooking* and *The Italian Grill.* She was also the editor of *The Magazine of La Cucina Italiana.* She has written for major publications including *Cooking Light, Fine Cooking,* and *Bon Appétit.* Micol Negrin lives on a small lake in New Jersey with her husband, Dino De Angelis. For more information visit www.rusticocooking.com.